Oz Clarke's
Wine Buying
Guide 2005

the essential companion to
Oz Clarke's Pocket Wine Book 2005

EBSTERS

timewarner
books

A TIME WARNER/WEBSTERS BOOK

This edition first published in 2004 by
Time Warner Books UK
Brettenham House
Lancaster Place
LONDON WC2E 7EN
www.TimeWarnerBooks.co.uk

Created and designed by
Websters International Publishers Limited
Axe and Bottle Court
70 Newcomen Street
LONDON SE1 1YT
www.websters.co.uk
www.ozclarke.com

Oz Clarke's Wine Buying Guide 2005 edition
Copyright © 2004 Websters International Publishers
Text copyright © 1992–2004 Oz Clarke

A CIP catalogue for this book is available from the British Library

ISBN 0-316-72784-9

Printed and bound in Spain

The information and prices contained in the Guide were correct to the best
of our knowledge when we went to press.
Although every care has been taken in the preparation of the Guide, neither
the publishers nor the editors can accept any liability for any consequences
arising from the use of information contained herein.
Oz Clarke's Wine Buying Guide is an annual publication. We welcome any
suggestions you might have for the next edition.

Editor Maggie Ramsay
Art Director Nigel O'Gorman
Editorial Assistant Davina Russell
DTP Consultant Keith Bambury
Production Sara Granger
Managing Editor Anne Lawrance

Cover photograph Nigel James
Cover painting David Dean

CORPORATE SALES
Companies, institutions and other organizations wishing to make
bulk purchases of this or any other Oz Clarke title published by
Time Warner Books UK should contact Special Sales on
+44 (0)20-7911 8117.

ADVERTISING SALES
Tim Bradshaw
112 Highfield Lane
Hemel Hempstead
HERTS NW6 6RD
tel/fax 01442 231131

Contents

Introduction

Forget Euro 2004, forget Tim Henman and Centre Court. Forget the bruised and bloodied rugby team, our cricketers, our oarsmen, forget them all. There is one thing for which we have every chance of matching the best in the world – and if global warming continues to favour us and enough passionate people decide to give it a go we can *be* the best in the world: sparkling wine. The quality of the grapes grown in Sussex by Nyetimber and Ridgeview is already up to top Champagne standards, the care with which they make and mature their wine is already way ahead of all but the most serious Champagne producers. What they need now is more people to join them, to plant the greensand and limestone slopes that spread impressively from the cliffs of Dover, along the South Downs and North Downs through Kent and Sussex, Surrey, Hampshire and Dorset, before quietly fading into the sea at Portland Bill – and an hour or two's ferry ride later resurfacing in France and heading for wine nirvanas like Chablis and Champagne.

> '...Côtes de Canterbury, Château Hastings and Domaine de Dorchester will become the sought-after cuvées...'

ENGLAND EXPECTS

I have to say, I wasn't surprised to hear the rumours from Kent that over a million pounds was furtively being invested in those limestone acres by several well-known Champagne houses. Quite right, *mes amis*. For great Champagne, you need limestone slopes and a cool climate. Your climate is in danger of becoming too hot. If the 2003 weather repeats itself on a regular basis, Côtes de Canterbury, Château Hastings and Domaine de Dorchester will become the sought-after cuvées for Champagne. Excuse me – not Champagne. That's French. From a strictly delimited area near Paris that has made the world's best sparkling wines for the last 300 years. That doesn't mean they'll make the best fizz in the next 100 years, or even in the next 50. The world's changing. The weather's changing. And those investments in the South Coast counties show the Champagne guys know it.

So who won our sparkling wine sections, not only in the Best Buys, but also in the Supermarket Selection? Ridgeview from Sussex. Whose new release this autumn will blast most Champagne out of the water? Nyetimber, with its 1996 Blanc de Blancs. Both leading the charge for glory and recognition for the English. The English are coming. And this time, no Centre Court nerves or penalty shoot-out panic will stop us.

NARROWING HORIZONS

But is our English wine world a thing of beauty throughout? No it isn't. In fact, several facets make me want to weep. As I write this, a battle is raging for the control of Marks & Spencer. A successful hostile takeover bid risks a decimation of the quality and individuality that marks out their food and drink sections, which have performed superbly in quality terms – and, I hope, in terms of profit too – over the last few difficult years. In our Supermarket top 20 last year M&S took four slots. This year they took five places, and were a success in every other category. Their wines have never been better. Will I be able to say that this time next year? They seem to have survived the first hostile bid, but their new boss has entered into a round of cost-cutting directed at suppliers which one producer said reminded him scarily of the cut-throat 1980s. Could all that hard work in quality improvement be about to go down the plughole?

And a year ago Safeway took five of the top 20 Supermarket spots. With wines like Merlot Visión, Montes Alpha Chardonnay and Errázuriz Syrah from Chile, and Alkoomi and Jim Barry Lodge Hill Shiraz from Australia. All stunning wines. All offered at less than a tenner. Are they still on Safeway's shelves? Well, there isn't a Safeway any more. This imaginative, innovative and, in my naïve terms, presumably profitable group has been taken over by Morrisons after a long, drawn-out battle. As far as we can tell, Morrisons are keen to take on the deep discounting big boys like Asda and Tesco, and last time I passed a Morrisons store there was a big placard proudly proclaiming '100 wines at £2.99'. That might be what Morrisons base their wine business on. But Safeway was different. Safeway was brave and pro-active and eager to try new things. Why couldn't its successful wine division have been left as it was? Are Morrisons really going to make more profit by maximizing their number of wines below £2.99 and slugging it out to the death with the master bruisers, Asda and Tesco?

Now, Morrisons do have some decent wines – half a dozen of their wines feature in this guide's lower price brackets. But what the Safeway debacle has done, and what any Marks & Spencer or indeed Sainsbury's – there are rumours about them too – takeover would do is to reduce choice for us wine drinkers.

Choice is what the UK used to do so well, right the way through our wine trade. You'd travel the world and legions of producers would talk about their enthusiasm for the British and their wine world. And quite rightly, London was talked of as the centre of the world's wine business. If you wanted to be anybody, you had to be somebody in London first.

The tales I hear now – in countries like South Africa, Australia, New Zealand and Chile as well as in France, Portugal and Spain – are of the ruthlessness of supermarket buyers, of the loss of interest in diversity and quality, and of an obsession with the deal, the deal, the deal. And if you don't offer a cut-throat deal on one wine, you'll find others of your wines de-listed without warning. You think there's less choice on the shelves than a year ago? That's one reason. It has got to such a state that some producers say they can't afford to supply the British market any more as they cut their profits to the bone and lay off staff. Increasingly, their better wines are going to other countries that are prepared to pay a fair price.

BACKING BRITAIN

But we can still save our own wine world, by not slavishly becoming discount junkies, not simply buying whatever is on offer, regardless of how it tastes. In every supermarket, upmarket *and* downmarket, there are good wines at a fair price that you *will* like the taste of. I beg of you – buy these wines, not just the latest 'Buy one get one free' of some junk you'd never normally let grace your table.

Now take a look at our Best Buys section (page 11). Look at the Top 20. Look at the variety of different wines we've chosen. Look at the prices for these fantastic flavours – most of them are under 10 quid. Then look at the names of the merchants. Bat & Bottle, Vin du Van, OZ Wines, Great Western Wine, Waterloo Wine Company, Raeburn Fine Wine – and well done Tesco and Waitrose for also being in this august company. But most of these are independents. These are the passionate enthusiasts who get welcomed with open arms when they arrive on foreign shores to search out new and thrilling flavours. They don't demand 'the deal'. They say – that's beautiful, what's a fair price? And when they've negotiated that hurdle, they come back to Britain and charge a fair price to us.

Every region of Britain has its independents. But then, by logging on to their websites, they could be next door anyway. If you live in Bristol but like the sound of wines from Raeburn Fine Wine in Edinburgh, log on to their website – they're all there. Or you could stay local and pop round to Reid Wines in nearby Hallatrow. And obviously you could turn up at your local Oddbins or Waitrose or M&S and pick out some of their beauties. But do consciously make the choice to buy wines you genuinely want, preferably from people who will genuinely enjoy serving you. If we make use of the choice we still have, in future years we'll still have that choice.

OZ Clk

Wine finder

RED WINES
VdP = Vin de Pays

Under £5
Altozano, Tempranillo-Merlot 68
Argentine Sangiovese (Somerfield), La Agrícola/Zuccardi 74
Argentinian Malbec (Asda), La Riojana 74
Argentinian Red (Asda), La Riojana 76
Australian Dry Red, First Flight 75
Bonarda-Sangiovese, Terra Organica, Zuccardi 88
Cabernet Sauvignon, Chilean (Somerfield), Viña Cornellana 73
Cabernet Sauvignon, Chilean (Sainsbury's), Viña Las Cabras 75
Cabernet Sauvignon, Chilean (Asda), Viña San Pedro 75
Calatayud, Garnacha Old Vines, Poema 39
Cariñena, Tempranillo 74
Carmenère, Casillero del Diablo, Concha y Toro 66
Carmenère, Los Robles 36
Carmenère, Misiones de Rengo 66
Carmenère, Paso del Sol 75
Claret, Patrice Calvet 76
Comté Tolosan, VdP du, House Wine (Marks & Spencer) 74
Corbières (Morrisons) 71
Corbières (Sainsbury's) 76
Coteaux du Languedoc (Morrisons) 71
Côtes du Ventoux, La Rectorie 73
Il Fagiano 38
First Flight, Australian Dry Red 75
Fitou, Cuvée Rocher d'Embrée (Somerfield), Mont Tauch 70
Fitou (Asda), Mont Tauch 74

Fitou (Morrisons), Mont Tauch 73
Garnacha Old Vines, Poema, Calatayud 39
Grenache, Peter Lehmann 37, 88
House Wine (Marks & Spencer), VdP du Comté Tolosan 74
Malbec, Argentinian (Asda), La Riojana 74
Merlot, Coldridge Estate 43
Merlot, Concha y Toro 37
Merlot, Casillero del Diablo, Concha y Toro 37
Merlot, Chilean (Sainsbury's) 75
Merlot, Paso del Sol 76
Merlot, Viña Sardasol, Navarra 42
Merlot, Sierra Grande 42
Merlot, Touchstone 36
Minervois (Morrisons) 73
Minervois (Sainsbury's) 68
Mourvèdre-Shiraz, Tortoiseshell Bay, Casella Wines 71
Navarra, Merlot, Viña Sardasol 42
Nero d'Avola-Syrah 90
Petite Sirah, The Boulders 68
Pinot Noir, Cono Sur 38, 89
Pinotage, Helderberg 69
Pinotage-Shiraz, Dumisani 71
Portada, DFJ Vinhos 43
Primitivo-Merlot, Da Luca 38
St-Chinian, Dom. St Laurent 42
Sangiovese, Argentine (Somerfield) 74
Shiraz Old Vine, Evolution 72
Shiraz, First Flight Reserve 70
Shiraz, Obikwa 43
Shiraz, Snake Creek 42
Shiraz-Cabernet, First Flight 71

Shiraz-Petit Verdot, Ransome's Vale 72
Syrah Vieilles Vignes VdP d'Hauterive, Dom. la Bastide 39
Tempranillo, Cariñena 74
Tempranillo, El Furioso 43
Tempranillo, Oak-aged, Valdepeñas, Félix Solís 71
Tempranillo-Merlot, Altozano 68
Valdepeñas, Félix Solís 71
Zinfandel Reserve (Tesco Finest) 70

£5–£10
Agiorgitiko, Palivou Vineyards 41
Alicante, VdP de l'Aude, Ch. Ollieux Romanis 15
Anjou Villages Brissac, Ch. la Varière 59, 88
Beaujolais, Jean François Garlon 34, 88
Bonarda, Alamos, Catena Zapata 64
Cabernet Sauvignon, Nativa, Carmen 18, 89
Cabernet Sauvignon, The Society's Chilean, Concha y Toro 30
Cabernet Sauvignon, High Trellis, d'Arenberg 89
Campo de Borja, Garnacha Old Vines, Campaneo 60, 88
Carignan Vieilles Vignes VdP des Côtes Catalanes, Dom. Baille 30
Chianti Classico Riserva, Ampelos 63, 90
Corbières, Cuvée Alice, Marie Huc/Ch. Ollieux Romanis 36
Côtes du Rhône Villages, Dom. de l'Enclos 33
Côtes de Castillon, Seigneurs d'Aiguilhe 52
Coyam, Viñedos Orgánicos Emiliana 12
Evangelo 40
Faugères, Clos Roque d'Aspes 30

Wine finder

Wine finder

Top twenty

One of the most joyful parts of preparing this guide is reading the wine lists of the truly independent merchants. Sometimes these will be well-established companies of real individuality, such as Adnams of Southwold, Yapp Brothers – the Rhône and Loire experts from Wiltshire – or the venerable but brilliant Wine Society. And sometimes they will be inspired, brave, idiosyncratic ventures like Vin du Van, OZ Wines or Bat & Bottle, small companies run with passion, imagination and, often, eccentricity. It is companies like these that keep spirits high in these troubled times when multi-nationals and retail giants seem ever more intent on establishing a stranglehold over our wine world. Such independent spirits make the fight for our wine future worthwhile.

Please bear in mind that wine is not made in infinite quantities – some of these may well sell out, but the following year's vintage should then become available.

❶ 2001 Cabernet-Merlot, Arlewood, Margaret River, Western Australia, £12.95, Vin du Van
I love it when I discover new properties in regions I thought I knew well. Where have these guys been hiding? And trust Vin du Van to rootle around and smoke them out of their lair so that they can cart a precious few bottles back to England. This is simply breathtaking wine. It does wear a kind of serious look on its face, like all Margaret River Cabernets do, but it isn't a scowl, there's nothing ill-humoured about it. It's just that this red has a truly classic depth of flavour – blackcurrants and black plums mixed with cherry marzipan; coriander seed scent rubbing along with crystallized violet leaves; and the texture has the softness of Danish pastry and a richness almost like syrup. And it's bone dry ... dry to its very heart.

❷ 2001 Coyam, Viñedos Orgánicos Emiliana, Valle Central, Chile, £8.95, Vintage Roots, Wine Society

Here is the shining face of the new Chile held high for us to admire. Alvaro Espinoza is a winemaker of genius, and he's also a

passionate believer in nurturing and caring for his land. And with quality sky high, he charges a very fair price for a great wine. He knows that a country's reputation is not made by charging more, it's made by delivering more. And in Alvaro, Chile has a great ambassador. In this wine he's married five different grape varieties so seamlessly that there's no varietal focus. There doesn't

need to be. It's a deep, dark wine, with some of the flavours still restless in the depths of this heavy, serious creation, which will continue to develop and expand for years – a warm, loving, argumentative marriage of grape flavours all wrapped in the cocoon of a great winemaker's passion.

❸ 2001 Cjanòrie, Emilio Bulfon, Friuli, Italy, £10.50, Bat & Bottle

Oh for more guys like the fantastic Emilio Bulfon, and more guys like Bat & Bottle to track them down! Bulfon makes wine in Friuli, the border area between north-east Italy and the mysteries of the Balkans. This area has been heavily colonized

by non-native grape varieties like Merlot and Sauvignon, but was once a hotbed of fascinating local varieties, reflecting its position in the melting pot of several disparate cultures. The inspired Signor Bulfon has managed to recover 24 different 'lost' grapes, some of whose pedigrees go back to ancient Rome as well as up to Hungary and across to Romania. Cjanòrie is an ancient local grape, with so much character and charm that it makes you wonder how much damage has the jack-booted march of international varieties like Cabernet and Chardonnay done across the world? You probably *never* tasted a red wine

like this. It is ridiculously fruity, like the juice at the bottom of a summer pudding, all loganberries and blackberries and strawberries. And I haven't even mentioned the scent: Turkish Delight, rose petals, rose water in a fruit salad, violet and jasmine. Don't resist the temptation. Scramble to buy. You may be helping to save one of the world's most delicious grapes.

For more wine recommendations see Oz Clarke's Wine Style Guide, pages 88–96

❹ 2002 Shiraz, Phillips Estate,
⚑ Pemberton, Western Australia,
£10.99, OZ Wines

This astonishing Shiraz is like no other Shiraz you'll ever have tasted. It smells so savoury that it seems like an inspired casserole of smoked mackerel soaked in the blood oozing from a rare sirloin steak, with mocha coffee and sun-dried tomato thrown in. Did I say it also has a Romaine lettuce freshness – and it's peppery – and it has a lush, seductive texture of sweet loganberry and blackberry and still manages to cram in some chocolate before finishing as fresh and tangy as tomato leaves? And have you dashed to buy some yet? Hurry, or I'll have bought it all.

---

❺ 2002 Semillon, Tim Adams, Clare Valley, South Australia,
⚑ £8.99, Tesco

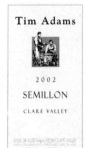

A great Aussie original. This is a haughty, almost arrogantly dry white, yet it has fantastic layers of flavour. It smells of custard apples, and it tastes of custard too, though the first sip seems to be all green apple peel and lemon juice. Gradually the flavour opens out into custard and warm bread crust and cake spice, but lime zest streaks through it. This is challenging and brilliant now. In five to 15 years it will be rich and soft – and unlike any other white wine in the world. The only normal thing about this wine is that you can get it at Tesco.

---

❻ 2001 Shiraz, The Willows, Barossa
⚑ Valley, South Australia,
£10.99, Australian Wine Club

The Willows is famous for producing hedonistic 'lie back and pour it down my throat' reds. Well this one briefly throws down a challenge. It may smell enticingly of cinnamon cake and Chelsea buns, but that first splash on your tongue has got a bit of attitude – black treacle and licorice and … and … – but then the challenge fades away and a glorious tastescape of dates and blackberries, treacle and spice spreads across your palate like a summer holiday sunset. *Also at OZ Wines.*

The Australian Wine Bureau is the generic marketing body for Australian Wine in the UK. We work hard at educating the public and the trade on the diversity and consistency that Australian wine has to offer.

For more information about our calendar of events and availability of Australian Wine in the UK please contact:

Australian Wine Bureau
Australia Centre
Strand
London
WC2B 4LG

the **australian**
wine bureau

www.australianwinebureau.com

❼ 2002 Shiraz, Red Edge, Jacksons Vineyard, Heathcote, Central Victoria, Australia, £17.75, Vin du Van

Vin du Van has discovered a sensational producer in Heathcote, which will become one of Australia's most famous vineyard areas – I mean it – in the next 10 years. Texture is the thing. The fruit is red rather than black, and that usually means the wine is a bit dry and lean, or light. Hah! That's the genius of Heathcote. The texture is fat and rich – and that's after smelling a metallic mineral austerity in its admittedly fruity aroma. The actual fruit flavour is of red plums – but then, the fruit is just a stage for the astonishing tastes of eucalyptus leaves and curry plant and well-hung bloody sirloin steak to dance on.

❽ 2002 Memsie (Shiraz, Malbec, Cabernet Sauvignon), Water Wheel, Bendigo, Victoria, Australia, £7.99, OZ Wines

This is just about the most irresistibly drinkable wine in the Top 20. By that I mean you don't have big discussions about this one, you just get it down you. And what you're gulping is a lovely rich red, packed with loganberry and blackberry fruit, softened by buttercream and scented with pepper and aniseed.

❾ 2003 Alicante, Vin de Pays de l'Aude, Ch. Ollieux Romanis, Languedoc-Roussillon, France, £8.17, Les Caves de Pyrene

The Alicante grape is banned just about everywhere. But in the right hands it can produce an absolute stonker of a wine – dark, blood red in colour, with a smell that tumbles out of the glass like sultanas and plums, allspice and meat on the grill. Taste it, and you get all that power; you think it might be too much, and then the wine does a delicate curtsey, offers you a lingering flavour of red plum and sweet pink apple, and then shocks you with the scent of jasmine.

❿ 2003 Sauvignon Blanc, Fryer's Cove, Bamboes Bay, South Africa, £8.99, Anthony Byrne

Bamboes Bay is just about the rarest, smallest, least-known area of South Africa. Hey, I've been there. There are very few

vines, they're blasted daily by the cold winds from the Atlantic – and they produce this superb, aggressive, crunchy gooseberry, lime and stinging nettle Sauvignon that will jump-start your taste buds at the first sip.

⓫ 2002 Shiraz, Heartland, Directors Cut,

♟ Limestone Coast, South Australia, £11.5, Great Western Wine, £13.99 Oddbins

Wow! This stuff is amazing. It's from a new vineyard called

Wirrega, pretty much in the middle of nowhere in South Australia, and all the Wirrega wines really do taste different. This Shiraz is as rich as you could want, packed with blackberry fruit and softened a little by toffee oak. But it's also infused with a remarkable penetrating scent of limes and the kind of menthol fire that would clear your sinuses on a wet Wednesday in Glasgow. The regular Heartland Shiraz (£7.95 Great Western Wine, £7.99 Oddbins) is also excellent.

⓬ 2001 Chardonnay, Diamond Valley Vineyards,

♀ Yarra Valley, Victoria, Australia, £10.99, OZ Wines

This is such an alluring wine. It's grown in high hills to the north-west of Melbourne's Yarra Valley, and last time I was there I watched entranced as kangaroos practised boxing at the edge of the vines. Which is as good a reason as any to like a wine. But add to the roos a delightful outdoor blossom perfume, a mellow fruitiness of eating-apple flesh and juicy white peach and more than a dash of oatmeal softness, and you have a very special Chardonnay.

⓭ 2001 Riesling, Waipara West, Waipara,

♀ Canterbury, New Zealand, £8.49, Waterloo Wine Co

This must be New Zealand's driest, most challenging Riesling, so any of you who see Riesling as a challenge in austerity, a sort of North Face of the Eiger white wine experience, well, get your crampons on and your ice pick sharpened, because this is marvellously taut wine, almost spritzy fresh, as zingy and sharp as piano wire dipped in lime – but right at the end there's just the slightest suggestion of honeybread and custard.

---

⑭ 2003 Riesling, Tim Adams, Clare Valley, South Australia,
♀ **£7.53, Tesco**

There's very little difference between this Riesling and the previous one, yet this, despite being one of Australia's driest, has a little more body and weight. But that doesn't interfere with the green leaf aggression, because this is green through and through – green apple, green pea, green lime zest, all sharp as knives to scrape your tongue clean.

---

⑮ 2002 Les Grands Augustins, Vin de Pays d'Oc,
🍷 **Tardieu-Laurent, Languedoc-Roussillon,**
France, £6.99, Raeburn Fine Wines

Powerful, challenging red that shows you don't have to go to smart areas to get great flavours. This is a mere Vin de Pays, and consequently not at all pricy, but it really packs a punch. It's reasonably tannic, but heaving with blackberry, sloes and black plum fruit; meaty; and strewn with handfuls of bay, mint and thyme.

---

⑯ 2001 Shiraz-Sangiovese, Il Briccone, Primo Estate,
🍷 **Adelaide, South Australia, £9.99, Australian Wine Club**

Joe Grilli at Primo Estate is one of Australia's most imaginative winemakers. It says Shiraz-Sangiovese on the label – already an interesting combination – but Joe has added Barbera, Nebbiolo and Cabernet too, and swirled them together to create a bone dry, very Italian style, with tar and black treacle and herbs, but also loads of blackcurrant and black plum like the best of homemade jams. *Also at Harvey Nichols.*

---

⑰ 2002 Pinot Noir, Quartz Reef, Central Otago, New Zealand,
🍷 **£17.95, Lay & Wheeler**

New Zealand is determined to carve out a reputation as the New World's greatest Pinot Noir producer, and all over the South Island – and in one or two bits of the North – there are promising sites producing a variety of different

styles. Central Otago – way, way south – is the most exotic location, high up near the snowfields, but the sun shines relentlessly through the cool mountain air and delivers rich-textured Pinot with a touch of tannin and lots of uplifting acidity, along with a sweetness of fruit like strawberry and red cherry syrup. *Also at New Zealand Wines Direct.*

---

⑱ 2002 Riesling, Gobelsburger, Kamptal,
♀ **Austria, £7.75, Wine Society**

Austria's white wines truly are some of the best in Europe, and her Rieslings equal those of Germany, as well as those of far-off Australia. Yet they're different in style. This has a perfume of honeysuckle that lets you know the wine won't be aggressive – and it isn't. Its fruit is like a really crunchy scented green muscatel grape; its minerality is mild and smooth; and its acidity is that of a very ripe lime blended with greengage.

---

⑲ 2002 Soave Classico, Pieropan, Veneto, Italy,
♀ **£8.95, Wright Wine Co**

It's not often I recommend a Soave, and certainly not at £8.95,

but there is change afoot in the lovely Soave Classico valleys and Pieropan is leading the charge. His Soave is a wine of genius: it has a waxiness that will turn to honey and goldengage in time, a revitalizing sprinkling of summer dust, and apple fruit so fresh and juicy you could have picked it from the tree. Wonderful freshness, yet no intrusive acidity at all. It's difficult to think of a white wine more satisfyingly easy to drink.

---

⑳ 2000 Cabernet Sauvignon, Nativa, Carmen, Maipo Valley,
♂ **Chile, £7.99, Waitrose**

If only all organic wine were this good we'd be queuing up to buy. Come to think of it, why doesn't Chile produce more organic wines like this, since its grapegrowing conditions are close to perfect? It'll happen in time, and while we wait, don't miss this beauty – the essence of blackcurrant juiciness seasoned with liberal dollops of mint leaves and eucalyptus gum. *Also at Butlers Wine Cellar, Oddbins, Wright Wine.*

Discover a new world

great
place to
make wine

Chile – the long,
thin country running
down the west coast
of South America –
is blessed with
perfect conditions
for winemaking.

Limarí Valley

Aconcagua Valley

Casablanca Valley

San Antonio Valley

Maipo Valley

Cachapoal Valley ⎫ Rapel
                  ⎬ Valley
Colchagua Valley ⎭

Curicó Valley

Maule Valley

Itata Valley

Bío Bío Valley

Malleco Valley

www.winesofchile.org

- VALPARAISO
- **SANTIAGO**
- SAN ANTONIO
- PICHILEMU
- RANCAGUA
- SANTA CRUZ
- SAN FERNANDO
- CURICO
- MOLINA
- CONSTITUCION
- TALCA
- SAN JAVIER
- LINARES
- CAUQUENES
- CHILLAN
- CONCEPCION

The Andes Mountain Range

Border

WINES OF CHILE

HARDYS

The best of Australia

—— SINCE 1853 ——

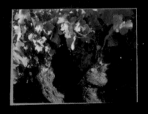 

Learning from the B E S T *of the past.*

Creating the B E S T *for the future.*

Handcrafting the B E S T *wines for today*

www.hardys.com.au

Runners-up

Another outstanding bunch of wines, really bursting with personality, once again showing you don't need to pay the earth for thrilling flavours. Although we have got a rather 'aristocratic' wine offering itself for sale at £29.45, half of the following 30 wines are under 10 quid.

❶ 2001 Villa Antinori, IGT Toscana, Tuscany, Italy, £9.99, Waitrose

Antinori is the most important producer of quality Tuscan wines, but I've frequently been underwhelmed by the quality. Not any more. At a recent tasting of the whole Antinori range, the quality and character was compelling. This is Tuscan red at its haughty best, with a deep, slightly fierce dry Sangiovese fruit sweetened and thickened into a lush dark syrup of black plums and blueberries and herbs by the addition of Cabernet, Merlot and Syrah.

❷ 2002 Shiraz, Water Wheel, Bendigo, Victoria, Australia, £9.50, OZ Wines

Victoria probably has more different styles of Shiraz than any other Australian state, and Bendigo, up in the goldfields, makes some of the ripest and most serious. This one has thrilling smoky chocolate and damson richness, blackened by licorice, scented with eucalyptus and mint and toughened up by a rasp of tannin.

❸ 2001 Pinot Noir, Waipara West, Canterbury, New Zealand, £13.75, Waterloo Wine Co

Waipara West never flatters to deceive; they make almost arrogantly austere wines (see also their Riesling, page 16). But the 'hauteur' of this wine doesn't mean it has *no* fruit – there's a positively intense strawberry and cream fruit and even some chocolate richness, but at the same time you feel as though you are licking the very stones of the vineyard.

❹ 2000 Meursault Premier Cru Les Perrières, Jean-Michel Gaunoux, Burgundy, France, £29.45, Lay & Wheeler

I wouldn't normally be encouraging you to spend £29.45 on a bottle of wine, but sometimes a classic with a hefty price tag comes along and I think perhaps they've earned it over the generations. If you want to know why people make a fuss about Meursault, the beautifully balanced oatmeal and acidity and hazelnut cream flavours of this still-evolving white Burgundy will give you some idea.

Aussie Shiraz

The Aberfeldy, Tim Adams (page 26)

Banwell Farm, St Hallett (page 63)

Bowen Estate (page 23)

Bush View, Evans &Tate (page 55)

Evolution, Old Vine (page 72)

First Flight Reserve (page 70)

Heartland, Directors' Cut (page 16)

Heritage (page 26)

Howcroft Vineyard (page 57)

Lunar Block, Kurtz Family Vineyards (page 23)

Phillips Estate (page 13)

Red Edge, Jacksons Vineyard (page 15)

Sainsbury's Classic Barossa, St Hallett (page 62)

Snake Creek (page 42)

Water Wheel (page 21)

The Willows (page 13)

SPARKLING
Banrock Station (page 78)

❺ 2002 Shiraz, Wolfkloof, Robertson Winery, Robertson, South Africa, £7.99, Sainsbury's
Shiraz is the sexy grape in South Africa right now, and it comes in all kinds of styles. This example has the softness of blueberry jelly babies and the richness of a stewed plum and damson pie dotted with ginger and citrus peel. Excellent now, sure to age.

❻ 2000 Ribera del Duero, Vega Riaza Crianza, Bodegas Valdubón, Spain, £9.99, Marks & Spencer
Although this may look expensive, it's actually a pretty cheap version of a very expensive wine. And it's good, with the classic 'salted butter on fresh bread' flavour of the oak, sensuously coating a dry but spicy and intense blackcurrant fruit.

❼ 2002 Vacqueyras, Les Christins, Perrin & Fils, Rhône Valley, France, £9.99, Tesco
The Perrin family own Château de Beaucastel, a famous property in Châteauneuf-du-Pape. They've also started a merchant's business, blending the wines of neighbouring villages, and they're proving to be very good at it. This Vacqueyras is typical – piles of ripe, dry, strawberry and cherry fruit and wild herb scent tacked on to a big, broad, meaty, country wine.

❽ 2002 Chardonnay, Buitenverwachting, Constantia, South Africa, £9.50, Wine Society
I still read reports from so-called experts saying that South Africa can't make great Chardonnay. I say she's doing very well, and getting better all the time. Witness this very classy number, restrained yet full of flavour, the toasted cashew and bread crust tastes of oak barrels expertly balancing the ripe dry apple and peach fruit.

For more wine recommendations see Oz Clarke's Wine Style Guide, pages 88–96

9 **2000 Shiraz, Lunar Block, Kurtz Family Vineyards, Barossa Valley, South Australia, £23.95, Vin du Van**

I'm not surprised it's called Lunar Block – the price is verging on the stratospheric. But these great Barossa behemoths can fetch silly prices at the moment and at least this one is seriously good grog, an amazing odour of menthol pervading the fruit, that veers from ripe to overripe and back and manages to mix cherry and plum with marzipan and raisins.

10 **2003 Pinot Noir, Lenbridge Forge, Yarra Valley, Victoria, Australia, £8.99, Marks & Spencer**

The Yarra Valley at its best manages to create wines of quite sublime texture and balance, even though sometimes I'd like a little more flavour. This has balance *and* flavour, with lovely pendulous loganberry and strawberry fruit, a scent of polished leather, and just a scratch of tannin and acidity.

11 **1997 Rioja Reserva, Baron de Oña, Spain, £12.99, Laymont & Shaw**

The Baron de Oña Reserva has been delicious for as long as I can remember – challengingly dry, but with a persistent strawberry ripeness mixed with vanilla oak that lasts for ages in your mouth. The 1997 is slightly less classic than some, tasting as though a splash of Bovril and a fistful of raisins had been added to the brew, but it's a fine wine – for now or for aging.

12 **2001 Shiraz, Bowen Estate, Coonawarra, South Australia, £13.99, Australian Wine Club**

Coonawarra is famous for Cabernet, but it also grows fine Shiraz, which used to be blended with Cab but is now increasingly released on its own. It's a lovely cool-climate style, but no less dark and intense because of that – Shiraz doesn't mind coolish weather – and the result is black fruit, black chocolate, black pepper and aromatic herbs in equal measure.

23

Other Aussie reds

Cabernet-Merlot, Arlewood (page 11)

The Fergus, Tim Adams (page 25)

First Flight Dry Red (page 75)

Grenache, Peter Lehmann (page 37)

Memsie, Water Wheel (page 15)

Merlot, Coldridge Estate (page 43)

Moppa Springs, Rockford (page 24)

Mourvèdre-Shiraz, Tortoiseshell Bay (page 71)

Novello Nero, Chain of Ponds (page 30)

Pinot Noir, Lenbridge Forge (page 23)

Shiraz-Cabernet, First Flight (page 71)

Shiraz-Petit Verdot, Ransome's Vale (page 72)

Shiraz-Sangiovese, Il Briccone, Primo Estate (page 17)

Tryst, Nepenthe (page 34)

Zinfandel, Nepenthe (page 52)

SPARKLING

Pinot Noir, Bird in Hand (page 45)

⑬ 2001 Semillon, The Willows, Barossa Valley, South Australia, £9.99, Australian Wine Club

Willows like to make crowd-pleasers and they consistently do that with their Shiraz (see page 13). Semillon isn't so easy, but this one is fat and waxy, with the texture of lanolin and toffee and with an urgent lime zest acidity and a splash of petrol. *Also at OZ Wines, Thresher.*

⑭ 1999 Cabernet Sauvignon, Max Reserva, Errázuriz, Aconcagua Valley, Chile, £10.59, Budgens

We don't often get the chance to taste mature Chilean reds, but they age very well, and this could easily last another five years. Right now the classic blackcurrant scent and flavour rock you onto your heels, the brooding black chocolate bitterness straightens you up again and the eucalyptus scent clears your sinuses for another go.

⑮ 1999 Moppa Springs, Rockford, Barossa Valley, South Australia, £11.85, Wright Wine Co

Though this comes from Rockford, one of the great traditional Barossa names, it isn't a Barossa blockbuster. This is a gentler expression of Barossa, with squashy strawberry fruit, a slightly home-baked feel and a wild herb scent – yes, a reflective self-effacing style in an age when many Barossa winemakers seem to have gone barmy for high octane.

⑯ 2003 Merlot, Winemaker's Lot 77, Concha y Toro, Cachapoal Valley, Peumo Vineyard, Chile, £7.49, Oddbins

If you were holding a masterclass on what really high quality, ripe Merlot should taste like, I'd recommend using this. It's made by Concha y Toro, from a very good single vineyard, and it manages to combine Merlot cake spice and soft, rich plumminess – which will turn all soft and buttery in

2–3 years – with a streak of stony dryness and a cautionary tweak of tannin.

❶⓱ 2002 Rioja, Arteso, Bodegas Ontañon, Spain, £9.99, Waterloo Wine Co
Not many Riojas nowadays use much of the ancient Graciano grape, but this one does, and it adds some extra grunt to the wine, not swamping the typical Rioja flavours of pastry cream, bruised strawberries and a hint of sultanas, but just putting a bit of muscle behind it.

⓲ 2002 Terra Alta, Torre del Moro, Spain, £7.69, Laithwaites
Terra Alta is inland from Tarragona, and not that far from Spain's priciest wine region, Priorat. It's a rough hinterland and you shouldn't expect anything subtle – but you do get brute power, intoxicating richness and real originality, as this stew of savoury basil and toffee syrup swimming with sultana, date and raisin shows.

⓳ 2002 The Fergus, Tim Adams, Clare Valley, South Australia, £9.99, Australian Wine Club
I always expect the Fergus to be a bizarre, not to say shocking, mouthful. So I suppose I shouldn't be surprised that this smells marvellously of dentists' pink mouthwash, a flavour that seems perfectly at ease with the torrent of herbs, raspberry and treacly fudge that accompanies it.

⓴ 2001 Montsant, Clos dels Codols, Spain, £7.99, Noble Rot
Montsant should be far better known than it is, since it encircles the mountainous redoubt of Priorat and makes similar wine for a fraction of the price. Grapes overripen here, so don't expect subtlety, but the flavours are balanced, and this rich, four-square red, pumped up with overripe plum fruit and smeared with a strange but delicious mixture of sausagemeat and coconut is memorable and *very* drinkable.

Aussie whites

Badgers Creek (page 76)
Chardonnay, Burra Brook (page 69)
Chardonnay, Denman Vineyard (page 55)
Chardonnay, Diamond Valley Vineyards (page 16)
Riesling, Tim Adams (page 17)
Riesling, Eaglehawk, Wolf Blass (page 38)
Riesling, Great Southern, Howard Park (page 56)
Riesling, Sainsbury's, Knappstein (page 70)
Semillon, Tim Adams (page 13)
Semillon, Peter Lehmann (page 29)
Semillon, The Willows (page 24)
Semillon-Chardonnay, Bin 77, Lindemans (page 38)
Viognier-Pinot Gris, Heartland (page 30)

SPARKLING
Clover Hill, Taltarni (page 45)

South Africa

WHITE

Chenin Blanc, Cape Promise (page 37)

Chenin Blanc, Ken Forrester (page 66)

Chardonnay, Buitenverwachting (page 22)

Chardonnay, Paul Cluver (page 27)

Chardonnay sur lie, Danie de Wet (page 42)

Sauvignon Blanc, Fryer's Cove (page 15)

Sauvignon Blanc, Peaks View (page 43)

Sauvignon Blanc, Porcupine Ridge, Boekenhoutskloof (page 39)

Viognier, Brampton (page 59)

RED

Pinotage, Diemersfontein (page 62)

Pinotage, Helderberg (page 69)

Pinotage, Lammershoek (page 28)

Pinotage-Shiraz, Dumisani (page 71)

Shiraz, Obikwa (page 43)

Shiraz, Wolfkloof (page 22)

SWEET

Sweet Surrender Pudding Wine (page 81)

Weisser Riesling, Noble Late Harvest, Paul Cluver (page 51)

21 2001 Shiraz, The Aberfeldy, Tim Adams, Clare Valley, South Australia, £19.99, Australian Wine Club

Aberfeldy comes from one of the great vineyards in South Australia, planted in 1904 and celebrating its centenary this year. It is frequently one of South Australia's grandest yet eminently approachable Shirazes. The 2001, however, is still in sullen mood – deep and sturdy with black plum, cherry and black olive fruit all eyeing each other warily, and herbs and bitter chocolate clasping any lightness of spirit by the throat. It's impressive and serious and needs five years, but has less heart than the usual Aberfeldy.

22 2002 Shiraz, Heritage, Barossa Valley, South Australia, £10.99, OZ Wines

Power. This wine is all about power. Perfume, subtlety and sensuality don't come into it. But it is a mighty wine, demanding your attention if not your affection – a serious black brute of licorice and tarpaulin, the rough rasp of pepper and herbs, and a brooding darkness that will take a few years to reveal its riches.

23 2001 Bourgogne Chardonnay, Alex Gambal, Burgundy, France, £11.50, Mayfair Cellars

After blasting your way through a selection of New World headbangers it's often a delight to stumble on something cool and restrained and elegant. Indeed the danger is that the difference from what went before will be so pronounced, you'll not give it a second glance. But this was too good to miss – cool, dry, almost lean, but with classic white Burgundy flavours of oatmeal and honey and that strange sexy sweaty thing the French daintily call 'sauvage'.

㉔ 2001 Le Soula, Vin de Pays des Coteaux des Fenouillèdes, Domaine Gérard Gauby, Languedoc-Roussillon, France, £19.99, Raeburn Fine Wines

Fascinating wine from the high wild hinterland of Roussillon down near the Pyrenees, and made by local maestro Gérard Gauby. He uses mostly local grape varieties that would have disappeared into a blending vat at the local co-op, but under his care they produce remarkable wine, successfully marrying such strange bedfellows as baked apples, buttered brazils and hazelnuts and yeasty custard and finally leaving an intriguing memory of terracotta tiles baked by the evening sun.

㉕ 2002 Chardonnay, Paul Cluver, Elgin, South Africa, £7.85, Christopher Piper

This Chardonnay is grown high up a mountain pass overlooking the great sweep of False Bay towards Cape Town. It's very cool, and the grapes struggle to ripen before autumn rains set in. Which sounds just like Burgundy in France. Well that's what the wine tastes like – gentle nut softness, toasted cashews and honeysuckle and noticeable acidity to freshen up your palate. An excellent example of New World fruit and Old World texture. *Also at La Réserve.*

㉖ 2003 Valdeorras, Godello, Alan de Val, Spain, £7.99, The
♀ **Winery**
What a delight! The rare Godello grape – I only taste one or
two examples a year – is one of Spain's hidden treasures.
Grown way up in the north-west, it is soothingly soft, with
gentle baked apple fruit and peach blossom scent, and there's
just a touch of that rasp you get when you chew the skin of a
fresh peach.

㉗ 2002 Pinotage Barrique, Lammershoek, Swartland,
🍷 **South Africa,** £9.85, Roger Harris
Lammershoek is a serious and fashionable new operation on
South Africa's west coast, where an increasing number of her
most original reds and whites come from. This is powerful
Pinotage, very true to the classic flavours of the grape:
mulberry fruit swirled about with toasted marshmallow and
coal smoke – but there's also a good creamy texture from
aging in oak and, being the aggressive Pinotage, a slap of
tannin too.

*'...mulberry fruit swirled about with toasted
marshmallow and coal smoke'*

㉘ 2001 Côtes du Rhône-Villages, Cuvée Nôtre Dame des
🍷 **Cellettes,** Domaine Ste-Anne, Rhône Valley, France,
£10.40, Haynes Hanson & Clark
We're seeing an increasing number of very classy red Côtes du
Rhônes from the previously neglected west bank of the
Rhône Valley – and here's one from a fine domaine better
known for its white wine. But this is top red with a big chunk
of the burly Mourvèdre grape contributing to a rich, solid,
unsubtle core – even the impressive plum and damson fruit
seems slightly bruised, the herbs parched by drought. Not
typical, perhaps, but dark and good.

㉙ 2002 Limoux Chardonnay, Château Rive-Blanques,
♀ **Cuvée de l'Odyssée,** Languedoc-Roussillon, France,
£8.25, Great Western Wine
Limoux, way down in France's south-west, is best known for
very good sparkling wine, but it is now promising to be an
excellent region for table wines, in particular Chardonnay.
The style is very soft-edged, smooth, round – almost New
World in its banana, cream and juicy pear mellowness, but
recognizably French in its evident acidity and restrained
spicy oak.

For more wine recommendations see Oz Clarke's Wine Style Guide, pages 88–96

㉚ 1996 Chardonnay, Vickers Vineyard, Idaho, USA, £13.50, Savage Selection

And now for something completely different. I know it's a Chardonnay – but it's from Idaho, a most unlikely mountain state in America's north-west, where you risk frost destroying your crop in spring and autumn. But the fruit that survives is remarkably good – with a virtual overdose of the savoury sausagemeat character the Burgundians called 'sauvage', a rich honey syrup blended with goldengage purée, as well as the drifting smoke of a cowboy's campfire, and a mountain acidity that, after eight years aging, has just begun to calm down and behave itself.

Under £7

This is the heartland for independent merchants. As soon as you break out of the £4.99 price point straitjacket, everyone seems to start breathing more freely, wines seem to garner more perfume and spice, the fruit seems to be richer, the personality more vivid. The biggest leaps in quality are from Australia and from France. Too much Australian cheap wine tastes rather limp nowadays, but force your way past the £5 barrier and there's an immediate improvement. With France, what you get is far more wines from single properties, even though they're often in unheralded regions. But that's a great recipe for value and flavour.

❶ 2001 Semillon, Peter Lehmann, Barossa, South Australia, £6.25, Flagship Wines

This is wonderful wine for the price. Semillon isn't a particularly popular grape variety, but in the hands of that great crowd-pleaser Peter Lehmann you get more character at the price level than with any other white. It's a limpid gold colour and has a fascinating smell of beeswax, strawberries and custard that simply gets better when you take a slug, and adds a lemony zest and a fistful of fresh roasted cashews to the medley before easing off into the ripeness of a fat peach on the point of overripening.

❷ 2003 Viognier-Pinot Gris, Heartland, Langhorne Creek, South Australia, £6.10, Great Western Wine
Another delicious Australian white, but completely different in style from the Semillon above. This is bright, fresh, breezy wine, blithely blending softness with perfume and smelling of apple blossom blown in the wind and tasting dry but succulent – a Williams pear, a white peach, the icing sugar on a chunk of Turkish Delight ...

❸ 2002 Novello Nero (Barbera, Grenache, Sangiovese) Chain of Ponds, Adelaide Hills, South Australia, £5.99, Somerfield
Fascinating blend of Italian and French grape varieties from high in the hills above Adelaide. Thrown together they create a bundle of explosively juicy fruit that seems positively sweet, it's so ripe. Black cherries, black plums and raspberries, with just a whiff of barbecue smoke.

❹ 2000 Faugères, Clos Roques d'Aspes, Languedoc-Roussillon, France, £6.99, Marks & Spencer
The character comes partly from the excellent hillside vineyards of Faugères in southern France, but equally important is the grape variety, Mourvèdre, which is rarely bottled on its own. It gives very four-square wine, not scented, but brooding and powerful, with a rich viscous texture of stewed fruit and a distinct tannic burr.

❺ 2002 Carignan Vieilles Vignes, Domaine Baille, Vin de Pays des Côtes Catalanes, Languedoc-Roussillon, France, £6.39, Laithwaites
Carignan is an ancient grape variety that is often treated with contempt by modernists. Well, they're making a mistake. When the vines are old – and they are here – Carignan produces tremendous wine, dark and dry, with a marked zesty acidity and woodbark roughness, but loads of plum and wine gum fruit, a delightful seasoning of bay leaf and thyme, and even a flicker of perfume in the aftertaste.

❻ 2003 The Society's Chilean Cabernet Sauvignon, Concha y Toro, Maipo Valley, Chile, £5.50, Wine Society
There's no other country in the world that delivers so much red wine flavour for the price. Chile just creams the

Laithwaites
FROM THE VINEYARD TO YOUR DOOR

SAVE 30%
on fine old-vine Chablis

A far cry from anything you might stumble across in the supermarket, Laithwaites wines prove that quality and flair can never be mass-produced. Our focus is on craftsman-made gems like this superb Chablis exclusive.

You won't find a more passionate champion of 'true' Chablis than Eric Dampt. Rich and deliciously fresh - his wine is a flawless example of one of the world's great white wine styles.

Order now while stocks last.

12 bottles for JUST £79.95
6 bottles for JUST £39.95
plus £4.99 p&p

"For 35 years I've been seeking out 'real' wines: those with the extra flavour and character to stand out from the crowd. Unlike supermarket big brands, real wines are made in small volumes by craftsman winemakers. You really can taste the difference!"

Tony Laithwaite
Chairman

opposition. And the giant Concha y Toro company is a superb leader for their wine industry, delivering this seriously weighty red packed with blackcurrant and black plum juice, but also seasoned with celery and soy and the scent of eucalyptus.

7 2003 Sauvignon Blanc, Holmes, Marlborough, New Zealand, £7.02, Vintage Roots

Lovely appetizing Sauvignon from New Zealand. And it's organic, which is not that common in New Zealand, because they seem to cower under a permanent threat of rain. Except that there are parts of the South Island which are very dry, and Marlborough is one of them. The extra care in an organic vineyard shows in the purity of flavour here – white peach and nectarine lushness sharply balanced by green nettle scent and lemon acidity.

8 2003 Merlot, Monos Locos, Concha y Toro, Central Valley, Chile, £5.99, Virgin Wines

Another offering from Concha y Toro, Chile's biggest wine company and, as usual, it's packed with vibrant fruit and sweet scent. This one matches the rich blackcurrant fruit with powerful savoury beef stew flavour and an appetizing perfume of fresh black peppercorns and juniper.

9 2002 Rioja, Cuvée Nathalie, Bodegas Muriel, Spain, £6.99, Co-op

How nice to find an affordable Rioja with some real oomph to it. I don't necessarily want Riojas to be blockbusters, but there are a lot of pretty feeble examples on the market. Feeble, this is not. In fact, it really needs another year or two to calm down and mellow, because right now it's a powerful, impressive brew of black fruit, cranberry acidity and pepper and clove spice, with creamy caramel oak struggling to hold them all together.

'...affordable Rioja with some real oomph'

10 2003 Jurançon Sec, Domaine Castera, South-West France, £6.25, Great Western Wine

Rare and fascinating dry white from way down in the Pyrenees. Jurançons, whether dry or sweet, have a great ability to hang on to their acidity. This one's dry, with an almost fierce apple and lemon acidity, and yet it also manages to offer a rich, waxy texture that makes for a unique glass of wine.

⑪ 2003 Sauvignon Blanc,
♀ **Explorers Vineyard,** Saint
Clair Estate, Marlborough,
New Zealand, £6.49, Co-op
Green, green, green. That's
what I want from my New
Zealand Sauvignon Blanc,
and I certainly get it here –
green apple and Kiwi fruit
freshness, lime zest and
green leaf acid attack and
mouth-filling but appetizing
dry texture.

⑫ 2000 Limoux, Chardonnay
♀ **Réserve, Les Quatre**
Clochers,
Caves du Sieur d'Arques,
Languedoc-Roussillon,
France, £7.03, Tesco
This comes in a ridiculously
heavy bottle, but so long as
you don't sprain your wrist
lifting it up, the wine's rather
good, with gentle ripe melon
and peach fruitiness, an
interesting suggestion of a bruise on the fruit adding rather
than taking away, and a smooth coconut creaminess from its
time spent aging in good oak barrels.

New Zealand

SPARKLING
Pelorus (page 46)

WHITE
Chardonnay, Wither Hills (page 93)
Pinot Gris, Villa Maria (page 63)
Riesling, Waipara West (page 16)
Sauvignon Blanc, Explorers Vineyard, Saint Clair (page 33)
Sauvignon Blanc, Fairleigh Estate, Wither Hills (page 33)
Sauvignon Blanc, Holmes (page 32)
Sauvignon Blanc, Shepherds Ridge, Wither Hills (page 55)

RED
Merlot-Cabernet Sauvignon, Villa Maria Reserve (page 89)
Pinot Noir, Montana (page 59)
Pinot Noir, Quartz Reef (page 17)
Pinot Noir, Waipara West (page 21)

---

⑬ 2001 Côtes du Rhône-Villages, Domaine de l'Enclos,
❗ Rhône Valley, France, £6.25, Averys
This estate is a bit closer to a nuclear power station than I'd
have liked – but perhaps that helps the grapes to ripen. Not
that they needed much help in the very good 2001 vintage.
It's also on the west bank of the Rhône – most of the Rhône's
good vines are on the east bank – and it combines rich
damson fruit with a scent of bay leaves and wild flowers and
a bone-dry streak of mineral dust.

---

⑭ 2003 Sauvignon Blanc, Fairleigh Estate, Wither Hills
♀ Vineyards, Marlborough, New Zealand, £6.99, Majestic
This is made by Wither Hills, one of the trendiest of all New
Zealand's wineries. They deserve their success because they
have made a string of top reds and whites. This is full-
bodied, but dry and zesty – no tropical fruit richness, just a
powerful statement of green apples, nettles and lemon
zest.

**⑮ 2003 Tryst, Nepenthe, Adelaide Hills, South Australia,
🍷 £6.99, Waitrose**
An inspired blend of Cabernet, Zinfandel and Tempranillo that
ends up as a serious glugger, full of crunchy ripe fruit, scuffed
by a bit of chunky tannin and savoury black olive, and scented
with hillside herbs and eucalyptus.

**⑯ 2002 Malbec, Faldeos Nevados, Mendoza, Argentina,
🍷 £5.95, Wine Society**
Argentina is only slowly realizing its potential, and many of
its signature Malbec reds are made in an 'international' style.
But this one isn't, even though it has a bit more toasty oak
flavour than I'd like. The violet scent sings out in the glass,
and the damson fruit is glycerine-soft and sweet.

**⑰ 2003 Minervois, Marielle et Frédérique, Château Tour
🍷 Boisée, Languedoc-Roussillon, France, £6.40, Waterloo Wine Co**
Perfume is important in Minervois too, though it can get
swamped by too much new oak. But not here. This is
relatively tannic in an attractively grainy way, but the fruit is
beautifully perfumed cherry and plum, which doesn't seem to
mind the tannin at all.

**⑱ 2001 Rioja Blanco Crianza, Linaje Vetiver, Bodegas
♀ Ontañon, Spain, £6.20, Waterloo Wine Co**
When I say a wine smells of pheromones, I sort of expect to
be misunderstood. But pheromones are very personal, and I
mean it has a rather sexy sweaty smell, glistening fresh sweat
caused by plenty of healthy outdoor exercise. Shall I go on?
Well, this is a serious bone-dry white, tasting of custard and
nut husks and slightly burnt rice pudding and a splash of
lime. And that pheromone thing.

**⑲ 2001 Minervois, The Renegade Dry Red No 1,
🍷 Languedoc-Roussillon, France, £5.99, Unwins**
Big weighty red, not particularly perfumed but full of
powerful stewed plum fruit and herb scent, with a stony
dryness to keep it appetizing.

**⑳ 2002 Beaujolais, Jean François Garlon, Burgundy,
🍷 France, £7.45, Roger Harris**
After a long day's wine tasting the last thing you usually
want is a glass of red. Unless it tastes like this – Beaujolais as
it used to be, the most quaffable, gluggable cherry-cheeked
red wine in the world. Sadly, most Beaujolais hasn't tasted
like that for a long time, but this easygoing glass of grog,
reeking of strawberries and bananas, scented with
sandalwood and pepper, is sheer delight.

Under a fiver

The £4.99 price point isn't such an obsession for the independent
wine trade as it is for the supermarkets. A merchant can talk to a
customer, get a relationship going, which rarely happens in
supermarkets. But £4.99 – or around a fiver – is a fact of life, and
we've discovered some good stuff here.

❶ 2002 Merlot, Touchstone, Rapel Valley, Chile, **£4.68,**
Vintage Roots
Wherever you look in red wines under a fiver, you're going to
find Chile over-achieving. This one not only tastes smashing,
but it's organic! You get a tremendous blast of black plum
and blackberry fruit but you also get a rich vegetable flavour
of old-fashioned stew, packed with celery, peppercorns and
soy sauce. I even thought there was some juniper there.

---

❷ 2003 Corbières, Cuvée Alice, Marie Huc/Ch. Ollieux Romanis,
Languedoc-Roussillon, France, £5.52, Les Caves de Pyrene
Corbières is a wonderful part of the world. Hardly any people,
high mountain passes, savage land that rarely lets you plant a
crop. Except vines. Vines can go where nothing else will grow.
Corbières wines usually have a magnificent, haughty, herb-
strewn flavour. But in 2003 the sun shone so hard that a
gentler side emerged, and this red is mild-mannered,
delightfully soft, awash with red cherry and strawberry fruit
and with a surprising floral scent that runs right through it.

---

❸ 2003 Carmenère, Los Robles, Traidcraft, Curicó,
Chile, £4.99, Sainsbury's and Waitrose
I've tasted this several times in the last few months and it
seems to taste different, depending on my mood. Sometimes
it's deep and dark and serious – richly flavoured, but stern –

and sometimes it seems positively fat and ripe. But whichever mood it catches you in, it'll have tremendous dark ripe fruit and the magic savoury pepper and soy sauce character of the Carmenère.

❹ 2003 Merlot, Casillero del Diablo, Concha y Toro, Chile, £4.69, Majestic
For price–quality ratio, you can't beat Concha y Toro. This is a wonderful mouthful of ripe plum and blackberry backed by serious, but not too serious, tannin and acidity.

❺ 2003 Chenin Blanc, Barrel Fermented, Cape Promise, South Africa, £4.49, Waitrose
South Africa is awash with Chenin Blanc. And if you ferment the wine in an oak barrel instead of a stainless steel tank, you'll get Chardonnay-like character at a fraction of the price. It's not quite Chardonnay: it's a little dustier, the creaminess is dry and nutty. But it's soft, satisfying and cheap at the price.

❻ 2002 Grenache, Peter Lehmann, Barossa, South Australia, £4.99, Flagship Wines
The juicy-Lucy Grenache grape handled by Peter Lehmann, crowd-pleaser extraordinaire – a recipe for happy juice. 2002 was a bit cool in the Barossa, so the wine is leaner than usual, and it's more peppery, more gritty, but there's still strawberry and eucalyptus fruit and the pepper is actually quite a buzz.

❼ 2003 Merlot, Sunrise, Concha y Toro, Chile, £4.99, Waitrose
Packed full of plum and blackcurrant fruit, with a challenging but delightful peppercorn and soy sauce savouriness.

Chilean reds

Cabernet Sauvignon, Nativa, Carmen (page 18)
Cabernet Sauvignon, Max Reserva, Errázuriz (page 24)
Cabernet Sauvignon, Viña San Pedro/Asda (page 75)
Cabernet Sauvignon, Concha y Toro/Wine Society (page 30)
Cabernet Sauvignon, Sainsbury's (page 75)
Cabernet Sauvignon, Viña Cornellana/Somerfield (page 73)
Carmenère, Casillero del Diablo, Concha y Toro (page 66)
Carmenère, Los Robles (page 36)
Carmenère, Misiones de Rengo (page 66)
Carmenère, Paso del Sol (page 75)
Coyam, Viñedos Orgánicos Emiliana (page 12)
Merlot, Casillero del Diablo, Concha y Toro (page 37)
Merlot, Monos Locos, Concha y Toro (page 32)
Merlot, Sunrise, Concha y Toro (page 37)
Merlot, Winemaker's Lot 77, Concha y Toro (page 24)
Merlot, Paso del Sol (page 76)
Merlot, Sainsbury's (page 75)
Merlot, Sierra Grande (page 42)
Merlot, Touchstone (page 36)
Pinot Noir, Cono Sur (page 38)
Pinot Noir Reserve, Las Brisas (page 60)

❽ 2002 Semillon-Chardonnay, Bin 77, Lindemans, South
♀ **Eastern Australia, £4.87, Asda**
A very nice traditional Aussie mouthful, with a custard and
breadcrust fullness and serious lime zest aggression.

❾ 2002 Primitivo-Merlot, Da Luca, Tarantino, Puglia, Italy,
🍷 **£4.99 Waitrose, £5.49 Budgens**
The Primitivo is a cracker of a grape, giving you gobfuls of rich
ripe fruit. It's calmed down here by Merlot – still deep, spicy,
smoky and plummy, but in a lighter vein.

❿ 2003 Chardonnay Les Argelières, Vin de Pays d'Oc,
♀ **Languedoc-Roussillon, France, £4.99, Majestic**
Just what southern French Chardonnay ought to be like.
Gentle and ripe, fluffy textured, with peach and white melon
fruit and the slightest lick of honey.

⓫ 2003 Riesling, Eaglehawk, Wolf Blass, Australia, £4.99,
♀ **Sainsbury's**
For a big brand like Wolf Blass this is not overpriced; £4.99 is
just right for a very attractive, soft, but lime-scented dry white.

⓬ 2003 Pinot Noir, Cono Sur, Rapel Valley, Chile,
🍷 **£4.99 Waitrose, Majestic, £5.03 Somerfield**
Year after year this is the best-value Pinot Noir on the market,
with far more flavour and personality than Pinot Noirs from
Burgundy at twice the price. Full, soft strawberry fruit, a little
glycerine fatness and a wisp or two of smoke. Delish.

⓭ 2003 Mâcon-Villages, Cave de Prissé, Burgundy, France,
♀ **£4.99, Waitrose**
I sort of did a double take when I discovered what this wine
was. Attractive fat apple flavour, a touch of perfume,
appetizing acidity, dry, round, eminently drinkable. And it's a
Mâcon-Villages? At £4.99? Of course, this is what Mâcon-
Villages should taste like, and this is what it should cost. It's
just that it hardly ever does.

⓮ 2003 Gavi, La Luciana, Araldica, Piedmont, Italy, £4.99,
♀ **Waitrose**
Gavi is often wildly overpriced, so to find a good example at
£4.99 is quite a surprise. It's a full but dry white with a lovely
fresh scent of lemon flower and apple blossom, with apple
fruit and lemon acidity nicely balanced when you drink it.

⓯ Il Fagiano, Bove, Italy, £4.95, Averys
🍷 This ripe, plummy earthy red, with a dollop of leathery
roughness, is spot-on Italian red. And it's from the Abruzzo, an

area that specializes in good, juicy, sturdy reds that are unmistakebly Italian and which, through its flavour-filled Montepulciano grape, is at last becoming a bit trendy.

⑯ 2002 Garnacha, Poema Old Vine, Calatayud, Spain, £4.99, Morrisons
Calatayud is one of the least-known of Spain's hinterland wine regions, and it is full of ancient Garnacha vines – the kind that make £15 wines in Australia. Here you get rich strawberry fruit, just a bit of baked raisin, and quite a lot of argumentative white pepper for just £4.99.

> ### Chilean whites
>
> Chardonnay, Viña San Pedro/Asda (page 75)
> Chardonnay, Casillero del Diablo, Concha y Toro (page 39)
> Chardonnay, Viña Morandé (page 73)
> Gewurztraminer, Sierra los Andes, Viña Carmen (page 64)
> Sauvignon, Santiago (page 43)
> Sauvignon Blanc, Viña San Pedro/Asda (page 76)
> Sauvignon Blanc Reserve, Viña San Pedro/Asda (page 70)

⑰ 2003 Sauvignon Blanc, Porcupine Ridge, Boekenhoutskloof, South Africa, £5.12 Asda, £5.49 Somerfield
The Western Cape, stretching up the western coastline of South Africa, is proving to be a fantastic cool-climate region in what is generally a fairly warm country. And Western Cape Sauvignon has a real tangy style: leafy perfume, green apple and lime acidity and a lean, cleansing finish.

⑱ 2001 Syrah Vieilles Vignes, Domaine la Bastide, Vin de Pays d'Hauterive, Languedoc-Roussillon, France, £4.99, Booths
Old vines really make a difference with red wines. The flavours are darker and deeper and more complex and often seem to get even better as the bottle empties. This is rich, almost overripe, but packed with enough black fruit and smoky scent for it not to matter.

⑲ 2003 Chardonnay-Viognier, La Chasse du Pape, Vin de Pays d'Oc, Languedoc-Roussillon, France, £4.99, Waitrose
Excellent example of how Viognier makes a great blender in the south of France. The Chardonnay fruit here is a little lean, but it's transformed by the apricot and pear fleshy freshness and the soft, lush texture of the Viognier.

⑳ 2003 Chardonnay, Casillero del Diablo, Concha y Toro, Casablanca Valley, Chile, £4.99, Majestic, Waitrose
It's not just reds that Chile excels at. This is lush, intensely fruity, but beautifully dry Chardonnay, full of fresh pear and apple fruit, balanced by keen acidity but broad and ripe in the mouth.

It's all Greek

Greek wines never seem to get the attention they deserve. Partly it's because the names and labels are difficult to understand – some of the labels are even in Hellenic script, which means that for most of us they might as well come from another planet. And partly it's because the flavours are genuinely different, which can make us a bit nervous at first sip. And, of course, partly it's because of retsina, the wine we all love to hate. Well, we thought that with the Olympics in Athens this year, the least we could do was try to persuade you to try Greek. So here's a selection of wines that are delicious – and really do taste different. Oh, and there's a retsina in there that, if its smell doesn't take you straight back to your summer hols, you have no soul. Or you've never been to Greece.

❶ 2003 Evangelo, Greece, £9.99, Marks & Spencer
Here's a supermarket superstar that's gone straight to the top of my Greek chart. It's made by top winemaker Gerovassiliou and he's taken some local grape varieties – I won't name them, it'll put you off your drink – and mixed them with the French classics Syrah and Merlot. The result is a sensationally perfumed wine – it smells of plum blossom and roses – and the perfume stays in the taste, which is creamy and plummy, juicily red with just a small scratch of tannic bitterness.

❷ 2003 Assyrtiko, Santorini, Hatzidakis, £9.50, Eclectic Wines (www.eclecticwines.com, 020 7736 3733)
Fascinating wine. Powerful, aggressive and blisteringly dry. It comes from a famously acidic grape grown in volcanic fields on the island of Santorini and – with its peppery bite and lemon-zest zing – you can almost taste the lava. *Also at Fortnum & Mason, S H Jones, Tanners, Wimbledon Wine Cellar, The Wine Society, Noel Young.*

> '...powerful, aggresive and blisteringly dry...you can almost taste the lava'

❸ 2003 Moschofilero, Theoni Mantineia, Stamata Attica, Domaine George Kokotos, £8.50, Yodeska (The Greek Wine Company, 01604 675522)
Wow! Have they been dunking chunks of Turkish Delight in

I've also chosen some Greek dessert wines in the section beginning on page 48

the vat, or what? This is beautiful, scented wine, soft as Turkish Delight, scented as a tea rose, yet kept fresh and mouthwatering by a sharp streak of lemon-zest acidity.

---

❹ 2003 Retsina, Cair, £6, Yodeska (The Greek Wine Company, 01604 675522)

Real retsina from Rhodes. This is like walking through a sun-baked pine forest. It takes you straight back to your holidays – the beach, the taverna, the taramasalata, the snooze, the sunburn. Perfick'.

> *'…like walking through a sun-baked pine forest. Perfick.'*

---

❺ 2003 Agiorgitiko, Palivou Vineyards, Peloponnese, £5.99, Eclectic Wines (www.eclecticwines.com, 020 7736 3733)

The Agiorgitiko is a native local variety, named after St George. It's a stunner, and has every chance of becoming a world classic in the next decade or so. It gives wines with a lovely soft lilt to them, floral perfume and the juiciness of red-fleshed plums sharpened by orange acidity and then sprinkled with a uniquely Greek combination of resin and mineral dust.

---

❻ 2003 Nótios, Gaia Estate, Peloponnese, £7.79, Oddbins

Another delightful, full-flavoured, bright, perfumed red from the Agiorgitiko grape. This one smells of bananas and fresh cherry blosom, and tastes of juicy red-fleshed plums stiffened up just a little by herbs and the dryness of wood bark.

---

❼ 2003 Moschofilero, Boutari, Mantinia, £6.15, Flying Corkscrew

Moschofilero can have an unbelievably musky scent – enough to have you calling for the smelling salts to ward off an attack of the vapours. This example is less extreme – nicely perfumed, but peppery too, with a sharp grapefruit flavour and thirstquenching stony dryness. *For other stockists contact Australian Wineries (UK) Ltd, 01790 755810.*

---

❽ 2003 Roditis, Palivou Vineyards, Peloponnese, £5.99, Eclectic Wines (www.eclecticwines.com, 020 7736 3733)

Roditis often makes up part of the retsina blend – in which case you'd have no idea how it was supposed to taste. But it can make pleasant white wines on its own, and although it's best known for maintaining its refreshing acidity in warm regions, this example has a pleasant apple crumble fruit, a glyceriny texture and soft banana split toffee finish.

Under £4

Booths and Oddbins both take this price point pretty seriously, and most of our recommendations come from them: the independent merchant often has ambitions further up the price scale.

❶ 2003 Merlot, Sierra Grande, Central Valley, Chile, £3.99, Booths

No country performs better at £3.99 in the red wine stakes than Chile. This has lovely rich black fruit, and a very attractive rather savoury earthy background.

❷ 2003 Chardonnay-Pinot Grigio, Riverview, Hungary, £3.99, Waitrose

Hungary makes Europe's best white wines at this price and no one does it better than the Riverview winery, where the winemaker has won top awards in the UK for his whites. This is a beguilingly gentle dry wine, with a soft apple and peach fruit just dashed with clover honey.

❸ 2002 St-Chinian, Domaine St-Laurent, Languedoc-Roussillon, France, £3.99, Booths

Very nice midweight southern French red, with juicy, jammy fruit and just a whiff of herbs. You can get deeper, more complex St-Chinians than this, but they cost a lot more.

❹ 2003 Shiraz, Snake Creek, South Eastern Australia, £3.99, Oddbins

Most cheap Australian wine nowadays tastes sweet – which isn't surprising, because they've started copying the Californians and leaving sugar in the wine. But this is refreshingly dry, with good plum fruit, a bit of spice, a bit of toffee softness – and a touch of bitter tannin to sharpen up your palate.

❺ 2003 Chardonnay Sur Lie Unoaked, Danie de Wet, Robertson, South Africa, £3.98, Asda

Danie de Wet's unoaked Chardonnay is year on year the best cheap Chardie going. He achieves its creamy softness by leaving the wine in the vat on its yeast lees; this gives a creaminess to balance the snappily fresh lemon peel and melon fruit.

❻ 2002 Merlot, Navarra, Viña Sardasol, Bodega Virgen Blanca, Spain, £3.99, Booths

Navarra used to be thought of as a kind of 'junior' Rioja. But it has its own personality, as shown by this burly, rich, jammy red with a buttercream mellowness to soften the attack.

---

7 **2003 Sauvignon, Santiago, Chile, £4, Noble Rot**
Pleasant, easy-drinking Sauvignon that combines a snappy leafy sharpness with soft ripe white peach and melon fruit.

---

8 **2003 Merlot, Coldridge Estate, South Eastern Australia, £3.79, Majestic**
Most cheap Merlots are pretty feeble, but this is the real thing – soft, wobbly-hipped, slightly stewy red plum fruit and no hard edges.

---

9 **2002 Shiraz, Obikwa, Western Cape, South Africa, £3.99, Oddbins**
Shiraz has become the sexy red grape in South Africa – which is no bad thing because the climate is ideal for it. This is nice and rich, with ripe red plum fruit and smoky toffee softness.

---

10 **2003 Syrah Rosé, Bellefontaine, Vin de Pays d'Oc, Languedoc-Roussillon, France, £3.99, Booths**
We're seeing a lot more Syrah rosés from the south of France as growers siphon off some juice early on in the fermentation to make more concentrated red Syrah wine. The siphoned-off juice ends up as very pleasant rosé: this one has a fresh, high summer flavour of strawberries and cream balanced by a nip of apple acidity.

---

11 **2002 Tempranillo, El Furioso, Viña de la Tierra de Castilla, Spain, £3.99, Oddbins**
Tempranillo is usually a little less angular than this, but Spain's weather in 2002 was tricky (as it was in the rest of Europe). The result is a red wine that starts out a little lean, but soon gains some dry strawberry fruit and finishes off with a taste of toffee and honey.

---

12 **2003 Sauvignon Blanc, Peaks View, Western Cape, South Africa, £3.99, Booths**
South Africa is really getting the hang of making crisp, tangy Sauvignon Blanc. This one verges on the aggressive, but I like its earthy brusqueness and tongue-tingling green leafiness.

---

13 **2003 Portada, DFJ Vinhos, Estremadura, Portugal, £3.99 Booths, £4.59 Unwins**
A consistent performer that always tastes triumphantly Portuguese, with its wonderfully original flavours of tea party cherry cake, kitchen spice and herbs.

MAISON
FONDÉE
EN 1812

LP

Laurent-Perrier

The Champagne
at the Chelsea Flower Show 2004

Fizz

We found a good mix of 'classic' Champagne and 'non-classic' sparkling wines from elsewhere in the world. Except that the most classic of all was the supposedly 'non-classic' Ridgeview from Sussex in England. We don't seem to have had much to celebrate this year. So let's celebrate English sparkling wines by raising a glass of Ridgeview.

❶ 1998 Cavendish Cuvée Merret Brut, Ridgeview,
West Sussex, England, £18.95, Jeroboams
Wonderful wine, everything you could wish for in a really exciting Champagne – except that it's not Champagne. It comes from the sunny downlands of Sussex. No problem. The chalk soils of Champagne are repeated endlessly in Kent, Sussex and the South Coast, and weather conditions are increasingly similar too. This cuvée is from 1998, so it's had six years to mature – important, since age softens Champagne – and it's now a thrilling mixture of dry mineral fruit, refreshing acidity and soft, soothing oatmeal creaminess. With bubbles. Excellent now, this will be even better in a year or two. *For other stockists go to www.ridgeview.co.uk*

❷ 2003 Sparkling Pinot Noir, Bird in Hand, Adelaide Hills,
Australia, £12.10, Tanners
Lovely fresh fizz. The French call this mellow pale pink colour onion stain or partridge eye – light pink with just a streak of orange. The flavour is of very ripe eating apples, so ripe they get a pink stain in the flesh, and stirred in with that is creamy yeast softness and a delightful caressing foam.

❸ 1999 Clover Hill, Taltarni Vineyards, Tasmania, Australia,
£14, Mayfair Cellars
Another wine that benefits enormously from a bit of extra aging: this is more than five years old. It comes from Australia's Champagne corner – the northern edge of Tasmania – and was a bit fierce when I first tasted it a few years ago, but is now delightful, balanced between fresh apple, baker's yeast and refreshing foam.

❹ NV Champagne Brut, The Wine Society's Private Cuvée,
Alfred Gratien, France, £21, Wine Society
I was beginning to wonder when we'd get to France, and I'm not surprised to see the plaudits being received by The Wine Society, because they get their own label from one of Champagne's all-time greats – the tiny, high-quality home of Alfred Gratien. This is still quite youthful and will happily age

for another five years, but it has a beautifully gentle style to it, dry but mellow, with an uplifting wavecrest of foam.

❺ 1996 Champagne, F Bonnet, France, £20.99, Oddbins
1996 was a great vintage for Champagne, but one in which the wines will develop slowly because the perfect ripeness of the fruit is balanced by high acidity. This Bonnet has evolved quite rapidly and the acidity is already well wrapped by nutty softness and a scented yeastiness that reminds me of warm brioche, fresh from the baker's oven.

❻ Franciacorta Brut, Majolini, Italy, £15, Bat & Bottle
This is a Champagne price – so it had better be good. Well, it comes from the inspired Bat & Bottle, so of course it's good! It's fat, rather rich, the apple fruit just pleasantly tainted with smoke and the yeasty softness gobbled up by foam.

❼ Crémant de Loire, Jean-Marie Penet, France, £9.65, Christopher Piper
Sparkling Saumur used to be enormously popular as a cheaper alternative to Champagne. It didn't taste the same, but the bubbles were good. This very pleasant Loire fizz has had enough aging to turn its green apple sharpness into soft eating apple ripeness drizzled with cream – and it *does* taste quite like Champagne.

❽ 2002 Gaillac, Mauzac Nature, Plageoles/Domaine des Tre Cantous, France, £8.70, Les Caves de Pyrene
This isn't at all like Champagne, and makes no attempt to be This is how fizz was in the old days – when they left the yeas in the bottle, like brewers of wheat beer still do. Talking of beer, this smells of hops, along with really crisp green apple peel, and the flavour is head-on juicy green apples – and that's just how Mauzac ought to taste.

❾ NV Pelorus, Cloudy Bay, Marlborough, New Zealand, £13.75 Majestic, £13.99 Unwins
There was a time when lots of Champagne tasted like this – full-bodied, creamy, mature. Very few do nowadays, because it takes time and money to create the complexity, the depth and the lovely nutty yeastiness that makes this inspiring sparkler.

❿ NV Champagne Fleury Rosé, France, £16.81, Vintage Roots
Very attractive soft but serious fizz. It's thoughtful rather tha celebratory in style and certainly not the stuff for chorus girl slippers, having quite a bit of acidity and a touch of bruising on the appley fruit, but it all combines very well into a full, ripe style. And it's organic.

⓫ NV Champagne Brut, Joly, France, £18.99, Flagship Wines
Another of those 'serious' Champagnes – ones which have a
real flavour and personality of their own and aren't just
buckets of froth. Most such Champagnes are from small
independent producers. This one does have a little bruised
apple fruit, but it's ripe and there's loads of biscuity, nutty
yeast in there as well.

⓬ NV Cava, Codorniu Pinot Noir Rosé, Spain, £7.99, Majestic
Codorniu have been the quality leaders in big-brand Cava for
ages, but I'd not given their rosé much thought until I tasted
this. I rather fell for its salmon pink colour and satisfyingly
ripe red fruit flavour all smothered with foam.

**⓭ NV Champagne Fleury, France, £18.99 Booths, £20.99
Waitrose**
This is relatively mature, being based on the 1997 and '98
vintages, but I'd still age it for a year or two more to let its
distinct acidity and oatmeally softness completely blend
together. Even so, it's very nice to drink now.

Fortified & sweet wines

The only kind of fortified wine that seems to be enjoying any kind
of vogue at the moment is the one which is actually the most
difficult to develop a liking for – dry sherry. Tio Pepe, whose brand
is probably the most famous dry sherry, have been sponsoring TV
shows like Gordon Ramsay's *Hell's Kitchen*, and seeing a healthy
increase in sales. But there's a lot more to fortifieds than just dry
sherry, and our selection this year digs out some real rarities.

**❶ Manzanilla Mariscal, Dolores Bustillo Delgado, Spain,
£6.65, Tanners [DRY]**
I've known this sherry for years and it is one of the most
consistently tasty dry sherries on the market. And this year I
almost wonder whether it isn't even better than usual.
Manzanilla comes from the seashore of Andalucía and people
often talk about the wine having a salty tang, but I seldom
find it. Yet here it is. Does it really have a taste of salt and
roasted almonds, or is that just what I'd want to drink it with?
It also has a slightly unnerving flavour of sour cream and a

For more wine recommendations see Oz Clarke's Wine Style Guide, pages 88–96

mature meat pie (don't ask!), but that's the way with sherry – the strangest flavours often combine into something remarkable and delicious, just as they do here.

❷ 2001 Botrytis Riesling-Gewürztraminer, La Magia, Joseph, Primo Estate, South Australia, £8.99/half bottle, Harvey Nichols [SWEET]

This takes a bit of time to get going in the mouth, but it ends up as a cracker. The Gewürztraminer might be flattening it out just a bit, because it is a pretty blowsy grape variety. But it's also very aromatic, and gradually a seductive scent of rose petals starts to pervade the wine and titillate the rich heather honey and peach and the taut acidity of the Riesling.

❸ 1997 Samos Anthemis, Greece, £8.75, Eclectic Wines (www.eclecticwines.com, 020 7736 3733), £8.75, Wine Society [SWEET]

The island of Samos has been famous for sweet wines made from the Muscat grape for centuries, but it isn't often that a fully mature one comes our way. The extra age in this has reduced its floral perfume and almost absurdly grapy sweetness, but in their place you get a rich barley sugar treacle mixed with pineapple, a delightful marmalade bitterness and acidity that manages to taste like orange juice.

❹ 1998 Semillon, Botrytis Affected, Tim Adams, South Australia, £8.99, Australian Wine Club [SWEET]

Tim Adams usually turns his Semillon into world-class dry white wine, but sometimes the autumn weather turns damp and humid and the Semillon grapes get infected with 'noble rot'. Which isn't much good for dry white, but it massively concentrates the grape sugar and makes for fabulous sweeties which mature beautifully. At six years old this is intensely syrupy, but scythed through with acidity so that you get all the flavour of Conference pears, and Bramley apples stewed with orange blossom, as well as barley sugar and fig syrup sweetness.

❺ Rich Oloroso Sherry, East India Solera, Lustau, Spain, £10.99, Waitrose [SWEET]

Syrup of figs again. That may bring back unwelcome memories, but think of the flavour of dried figs, then splash rich grapy syrup all over them and you get the idea. And it's not just figs. This wine is a blend of old dry sherry and old sweet sherry; the dry sherry brings a caramel nuttiness like buttered brazils and a roughness like hazelnut husks and the sweet sherry brings raisins and dates, sultanas and, yes... figs in syrup. *Also at many Sainsbury's.*

❻ Madeira, Sercial, 10 Years Old, Henriques & Henriques, Portugal, £16.99/50cl, Waitrose [DRY]

A lot of money – and you don't even get a full bottle – but this is a true original. Henriques & Henriques took one look at the dwindling Madeira trade and decided the only way forward was to become passionate about quality and *style*. Style is so important. There are four main styles of Madeira, going from rich, smoky, sweet Malmsey to stingingly dry Sercial. Stingingly dry, yes, but not lean. The acidity is searingly high and might make you fear for the enamel on your teeth if it weren't wrapped around with a positively unctuous nut-rich texture. And the fruit flavours are unlike any you normally taste in wine – persimmons, pomegranates and medlars. Old fashioned fruits. *Very* old fashioned wine.

❼ 1998 The Society's LBV – Late Bottled Vintage Port, Portugal, £9.50, Wine Society [SWEET]

Most so-called LBV is a rich, pretty tasty port that apes vintage styles from a distance. But one or two companies try harder, choosing top-quality base wine, aging it for six years in barrels, not filtering it before bottling – and Smith Woodhouse is the king of these. This Late Bottled Vintage is gentle yet peppery, rich yet not massively rich, fruity, yet not massively fruity, mineral yet not massively… in other words, balanced, satisfying, interesting, and ready to drink.

❽ 10 Years Old Tawny Port, Portugal, £16.40, Reid Wines [SWEET]

Tawny port gets its character from spending time in barrel, gradually losing ferocity and power and colour and gaining a mellow warmth to go with the russet-tinged hazelnut colour it has developed. This is a very attractive, easygoing, old leather armchairs and convivial banter sort of wine, tasting of dried apricots, dried figs, hazelnuts and heartsease.

❾ Mavrodaphne of Patras, Patraiki Wines, Peloponnese, Greece, £12, Yodeska (The Greek Wine Company, 01604 675522) [SWEET]

A real period piece. A wild and rather beautiful cross between oloroso sherry and tawny port, impressively rich yet assertively dry, full of treacle and dark brown fruit yet with an exhilarating sour acidity humming through its heart.

❿ Muscat, Rutherglen, Campbells, Victoria, Australia, £7.99, Oddbins [SWEET]

I managed to visit Campbells this year and gazed in awe at how incredibly traditional and old-fashioned everything is. I was also struck by how intimately involved with the final product these Rutherglen guys are. We tinkered with the blend, adding a dash of old, a dash of new, some big barrel, some small, some tiny – and completely reinventing the wine, so that you get this exotic, viscous essence of the Muscat grape, dripping with the sweetness of dates, sultanas, dried figs and moist muscovado sugar.

⓫ Tokay, Heritage Wines, Australia, £19.99, Australian Wine Club [SWEET]
Another of Australia's fortified gems. Tokay is made from the Muscadelle grape and isn't as rich or exotic as Liqueur Muscat. Some people like it more than Muscat, I don't like it quite as much – but you make up your own minds! Sweet date fruit, cake richness and a fascinating tea leaf and fish oil aroma should help you decide.

⓬ Vinsanto, Hatzidakis, Greece, £12.50/half bottle, Eclectic Wines (www.eclecticwines.com, 020 7736 3733) [SWEET]
Here's one for the brave. Vinsanto is a very ancient wine style from the island of Santorini. Sure it's sweet – but the excitement comes from the shocking sourness that cuts like balsamic vinegar through the rich but bruised flavour of old dates and raisins long steeped in syrup.

⓭ 2001 Weisser Riesling, Noble Late Harvest, Paul Cluver, Elgin, South Africa, £7, Christopher Piper [SWEET]
Although this wine is fairly sweet, the acidity is the most memorable part, and the taste is like an intense Bramley apple purée that drives its wedge of flavour remorselessly to the back of your mouth.

⓮ Palo Cortado Sherry, Harveys, Spain, £10.95, Wine Society [DRY]
This starts out with a fantastic flavour of caramel and melted butter – like buttered brazils that have been drizzled with melted salted farmhouse butter. And it's nutty, too, and scented with old orange peel, but as this promise of riches slides over your palate and slithers down your throat it seems to gather a mossy dampness which spoils it just a little.

⓯ Napoleon Dry Oloroso Sherry, Vinicola Hidalgo, Spain, £7.85, Christopher Piper [DRY]
A little gentler than I want. It does have good nutty richness, dry but ripe, and good, slightly sour acidity, but I search in its old bones for the stirrings of Napoleon's bygone imperial age and what I find is more like the comfortable but less daunting pleasure of a fusty old leather sofa in a *sous-préfecture* in the Auvergne.

Supermarket superstars

Things are a bit chaotic in the supermarket world at the moment, with the sad demise of Safeway and consequently the loss of a really interesting range of wines. Add to that the uncertainty over Marks & Spencer and you can understand why I'm feeling a bit edgy. But that doesn't mean there isn't still some superb stuff on the shelves, with three supermarkets in particular showing you can excel as well as offer a bargain. Waitrose has been smashing for years, but M&S are getting better all the time, and it is encouraging to see big boy Tesco, king of the price cuts, prepared to stock at least a few of its shelves with top stuff. And the prices are good. Only five of our top 20 were over 10 quid.

Please bear in mind that wine is not made in infinite quantities – some of these may well sell out, but the following year's vintage should then become available.

❶ 2001 Côtes de Castillon, Seigneurs d'Aiguilhe, Château d'Aiguilhe, Bordeaux, France, £7.99, Waitrose
If only there were more producers in Bordeaux like these guys. This isn't their top property. This isn't even their top wine from this property. But it gives you everything you want from Bordeaux, never overstating, not smothering you with flavour and intensity, but graciously setting out a seriously delightful taste experience. It manages to be rich, round and ripe, yet also appetizingly dry, its spicy oak delightfully balancing the cool, just-picked black cherry and black plum fruit.

JOINT WINNER

❶ 2002, Zinfandel, Nepenthe, Adelaide Hills, South Australia, £14.99, Sainsbury's
I was so thrilled by the 2000 vintage of this wine that this year I actually went out to Nepenthe, high up in the hills above Adelaide, to try to work out how they did it. It was a beaut trip, but I'm none the wiser. The Adelaide Hills are cool and damp, just right for snappy white grapes like Sauvignon Blanc. But Zinfandel is a big, hot-climate beast. How can it possibly ripen amid the mist and drizzle of the Hills? Not that I care, I'm just curious – and I suppose if I keep on visiting, one day they'll tell me. OK – the wine. Sensational. It isn't quite as rich and exotic as the 2000, but is perhaps a touch more approachable by ordinary mortals. Oh, I don't

For more wine recommendations see Oz Clarke's Wine Style Guide, pages 88–96

ALDI

At Aldi we are constantly searching for wines that will be technically well made, have typicity of fruit characters and for each wine to have its own personality expressing its terroir. We have extended our range by 20% in line numbers with each wine fulfilling our criteria.

Amongst the new wines are a lightly oaked citrus flavoured Semillon Chardonnay and a full bodied Shiraz Cabernet with spice and berry notes, both from **Argentina** and amazing value at **£2.99**.

Our **Australian** selection comprises of Mayrah Estates Chardonnay and Cabernet Sauvignon, Ransome's Vale Shiraz Petit Verdot and an enormous Evolution Old Vine Shiraz. All of these wines won awards at the International Wine Challenge and are all available for less than **£3.99**.

We haven't forgotten that the old world can offer great quality and value. Our single estate Pinot Grigio from the Veneto is a bargain at **£3.99** and our Claret, which comes from individually selected Chateaux, is great value at **£2.99**. Fine wines are available during the festive season with wines from three Bordeaux Cru Classé Chateaux and a Premier Cru Champagne, all at incredible prices.

The wine range in our stores is only one part of the Aldi offer
Come along and see what else is new

BRINGING MORE TO THE TABLE

know – because there's simply no wine in Australia like it. It's unnervingly rich, with all Zinfandel's typical fig syrup, date and brown sugar richness – but at Nepenthe they seem to shovel in loganberries and strawberries too, fistfuls of herbs and damp leaves (think of autumn) and finish it off with a sweet-sour flavour like leather splashed with lime juice. As I said – nothing like it. *Also at Stratford's, High Street, Cookham, Berkshire SL6 9SQ (01628 810606).*

❸ 2002 Rioja, Torresoto, Companía Vinícola del Norte de Espana, Spain, £5.99, Marks & Spencer

This is not a wine for the sensualist. It doesn't woo you, overpower you with scent, make your eyelids droop with its bulbous ripeness. It's more a wine for the ascetic, for the intellectual who has thoughts and ideas to pluck from his teeming mind and place in some quiet, logical symmetry. But if none of that makes sense, let's try another tack. Good white Rioja is one of the driest yet most individual whites in Europe, managing to hint at richness while the wine's raging dryness rampages over your palate. But hold on to those hints of richness, curious though they may be. Does the idea of custard, lime and lanolin attract you? Nut husks dipped in orange, ships' biscuits dry from years of criss-crossing the Tropics? Still doesn't make sense? I'm not surprised. White Rioja is a difficult but remarkable wine and the longer you ponder, the drier, yet the richer the wine becomes.

❹ 2000 Meursault, Louis Josse, Burgundy, France, £18.99, Tesco Finest

I know the guys who make this wine. They can give you sublime stuff, and they can give you dross. And charge you the same price. It's all down to whether they like you or not. Well, the winebuying team at Tesco (female, by the way) have worked their charms on these Burgundy boys and come up with a classic Meursault – gentle but full, totally dry and mixing Brazil nuts with oatmeal then coating them with ever-so-slightly sour crème fraîche.

> *'…classic Meursault…mixing Brazil nuts with oatmeal then coating them with crème fraîche'*

❺ 2001 Toro, Finca Sobreno Crianza, Spain, £7.25, Waitrose

In a country that is making an increasing amount of excellent value-for-money red, Toro is a powerhouse. I think the sheer fury of its fruit put off some of the fainthearted souls who form opinion. But not me. This is thrilling and original stuff. It's dry, impenetrably dark, throbbing with blueberry and blackberry syrupy fruit, with pepper to warn the palate not to relax, and a coconutty oak flavour that fades rather brilliantly into a savoury taste of parsley butter.

> '...impenetrably dark, throbbing with blueberry and blackberry fruit'

6 **2003 Sauvignon Blanc, Shepherds Ridge,** Marlborough, New Zealand, **£8.99,** Marks & Spencer

This is made by Wither Hills, one of New Zealand's top outfits, and this is absolutely classic Kiwi Sauvignon, with an unashamed flavour of gooseberry and capsicum, a green leaf rasp and scything lime acidity, softened by coffee bean scent. Full-bodied too.

7 **2002 Riesling Spätlese, Kirchenstück, Künstler,** Rheingau, Germany, **£13.99,** Waitrose

This was a really difficult wine to mark, especially at this fairly hefty asking price. At the moment it tastes half-formed – as though the grape juice and honey, acidity and minerals are all unsure as to how to marry. But these wines age wonderfully. If anyone out there is prepared to buy a bottle and leave it 5–10 years (yes, that long), this will be a supreme, honeyed, peachy wine streaked with minerals and freshened by an acidity that never seems to fade.

8 **2002 Shiraz, Bush View,** Evans & Tate, Margaret River, Western Australia, **£7.99,** Marks & Spencer

With typical M&S wizardry, they've managed to squeeze a Shiraz out of one of Western Australia's leading producers that is actually better than the one it sells under its own label. So, take advantage! This is quite reserved, with a fair nip of tannin and acidity, but there's also ripe rich blackberry fruit and it's already starting to develop licorice and black chocolate flavours that will make it even better in a year or two.

9 **2002 Chardonnay Reserve, Denman Vineyard,** Hunter Valley, New South Wales, Australia, **£7.99,** Tesco Finest

This is the type of Chardonnay that we don't see much any more. But it's what first made Australian wine famous – Hunter Valley Chardonnay, from near Sydney – waxy, smelling of leather that's been polished with oil, pineapple chunks from the tin, and custard burnt at the edges under the grill. Reading that, you may think thank goodness we've moved on. But in a modern world where too many Aussie Chardies taste dull and sugary, this is the real thing.

⑩ 2001 Minervois La Livinière, les Vieilles Vignes, Château Maris, Languedoc-Roussillon, France, £8.99, Waitrose

Minervois is a pretty big area in southern France. It's good: produces lots of tasty wine. But there's one part that has always produced the best wine, one little huddle of vineyards whose wines have always been deeper and darker: La Livinière. And this wine shows why it's special. The vines are 80-year-old Carignan and they're farmed biodynamically. Carignan is a slightly sullen grape – it rarely leaps out of the glass – so pour this wine and then give it a little time. You'll be rewarded with the scent of violets and thyme and a rich, syrupy, almost overcooked flavour of loganberries and pepper that is impressive rather than beautiful.

⑪ 2001 Gigondas, Cuvée Les Tendrelles, Les Espalines, Rhône Valley, France, £12.99, Waitrose

Waitrose is clearly making a big effort in the south of France, because here's another winner. Many of France's best reds are coming from the far south and the Rhône Valley; Gigondas is in the Rhône, just next to Châteauneuf-du-Pape, and it makes famously weighty wines that somehow manage to retain a bit of perfume. This is thick and syrupy, like a cherry-flavoured cough medicine, but there's also the brash attack of rosemary and thyme sprigs ripped from the hot hillside and a grainy tannic bitterness that makes for a powerful mouthful – not for the fainthearted.

⑫ 2002 Chablis, Cuvée Claude Dominique, Burgundy, France £8.99, Tesco Finest

A lot of commercial Chablis is rather flat and bland – and sells for several quid less than this. Tesco Finest makes trading up worthwhile, because this is anything but bland. It's very dry, with a meaty, oatmeal flavour of yeast that the French call 'sauvage' and a strong streak of minerals, as though the vines have their roots deep in the mother lode.

⑬ 2003 Riesling, Great Southern, Howard Park, Western, Australia, £5.49, Tesco

Have I persuaded you to give Riesling a go yet? If you're still nervous about trying something you think of as being sickly and sweetish from Germany or central Europe – well, real Riesling couldn't be more different. It's one of the most mouthwatering, bone-dry wines in the world, not that dissimilar in style to a good Sauvignon Blanc. Australia leads the world in making snappy dry Riesling, and this one, from a top winery in Western Australia, is laden with the scent of mint and anise and has a super-refreshing flavour of ripe apples and lemon zest. And it *is* dry.

⑭ 2001 Minervois La Livinière, Domane des Garennes,
Languedoc-Roussillon, France, £9.99, Marks & Spencer
If you think this is a bit expensive for a Minervois, just try the
wine and you'll change your mind sharpish. But this isn't any
old Minervois. For a start it comes from La Livinière, the very
heart of the region and home of the most scented wines. And
it's also a single-vineyard wine, dominated by the classy Syrah
grape. The grape quality bursts out of the glass with clouds of
violet and cherry blossom scent tangled up with bay leaf and
thyme. When you taste it, add a rich, smoky damson fruit to
the equation, and you've got a star wine.

> *'...clouds of violet and cherry blossom scent*
> *tangled up with bay leaf and thyme'*

⑮ 2001 Priorat, Coma Vella, Mas d'en Gil, Spain, £15.99,
Waitrose
Priorat is an ancient, rocky vineyard area near Barcelona
whose wines have become exceedingly trendy recently. That
means they've become much more expensive. But they've
also improved – and that often doesn't happen when a wine
becomes too popular. The style is overripe, almost OTT, but it
is hot down there, the yields are tiny, and the grapes bake.
You can taste it: the wine smells of caramel dates and prunes
and tastes like a thick, deep syrup of dried fruits from a
Christmas cake together with dates and glacé cherries. And
it's dry.

⑯ 2002 Shiraz, Howcroft Vineyard, Limestone Coast,
South Australia, £7.99, Tesco Finest
Shiraz grows all over Australia and the wines come in
numerous different styles. So it's nice when a new area starts
to make waves. The Limestone Coast spreads across the
bottom of South Australia, and it's packed with limestone,
one of the grapevine's favourite soils. This Shiraz is
beautifully ripe, with lots of licorice and toffee and plum
syrup richness splashed with spices, but the final effect is
appetizingly dry.

⑰ 2002 Ribera del Duero, Tempranillo, Vega de Castilla,
Spain, £7.49, Waitrose
This is excellent wine that ideally needs a year or two's extra
aging, because it's still slightly raw at the edges. Even so, the
flavour's so good – a cocoa bean and carob richness, vanilla
toastiness and deep loganberry fruit – that I *must*
recommend it, even if I'd hide it under the stairs for a
year or two.

Spain

WHITE

Rioja, Linaje Vetiver, Bodegas Ontañon (page 34)
Rioja, Torresoto, CVNE (page 54)
Valdeorras, Godello, Alan de Val (page 28)

RED

Altozano, Tempranillo-Merlot (page 68)
Cariñena, Gran Tempranillo (page 74)
Garnacha, Old Vines, Poema, Calatayud (page 39)
Garnacha Old Vines, Campaneo, Campo de Borja (page 60)
Merlot, Viña Sardasol, Navarra (page 42)
Montsant, Clos dels Codols (page 25)
Priorat, Como Vella, Mas d'en Gil (page 57)
Ribera del Duero, Vega de Castilla (page 57)
Ribera del Duero, Vega Riaza, Bodegas Valdubón (page 22)
Rioja, Arteso, Bodegas Ontañon (page 25)
Rioja, Cuvée Nathalie, Bodegas Muriel (page 32)
Rioja, Tomas Blanco Crespo, Telmo Rodríguez (page 58)
Rioja Reserva, Baron de Oña (page 23)
Rioja Reserva, Viña Caña (page 63)
Rioja Reserva, Viña Mara, Bodegas Berberana (page 60)
Syrah, Marques de Griñon, Dominio de Valdepusa (page 62)
Tempranillo, El Furioso (page 43)
Terrra Alta, Torre del Moro (page 25)
Toro, Finca Sobreño (page 54)
Valdepeñas, Félix Solís (page 71)

⑱ 2003 Touriga Nacional, Portugal, £5.99, Tesco Finest
Portugal produces some of the best-value red wines in Europe, with truly individual, defiantly different flavours. Touriga Nacional is a smashing grape, and this is a single-vineyard wine from an estate ringed by eucalyptus trees – and you can just catch a taste of eucalyptus snuggled in among the blueberry cream and blackberry-crumble-with-custard richness of the wine.

⑲ 2001 Molise Rosso, Vigna Ottieri, Italy, £6.99, Waitrose
Molise is one of the most obscure parts of Italy's wine world, so well done Waitrose for tracking down any of its wine. This has a really good, almost stewy red plums and toffee flavour, with that unique Italian bitter edge that here tastes like a lick of tree bark.

⑳ 2001 Rioja, Tomas Blanco Crespo, Telmo Rodríguez, Spain, £6.99, Marks & Spencer
M&S have contracted Spain's brightest young winemaker to help create their own-label wines. It's working, because while a lot of Rioja is overpriced and doesn't taste of anything very much except wooden planks, this example beautifully balances dry strawberry fruit and the dry but soft effect of barrel aging, with a fascinating palette of herb flavours: caraway, purple basil and that purple leaf they used to crystallize and put on cakes.

High street heroes

This second tier of Supermarket wines shows the depth of choice that the supermarkets can offer at fair prices. Only one of these 20 wines is over £10 and over half of them are below £7. The quality is there on the shelves, but we must go on buying the interesting wines, or the stores will stop stocking them.

❶ 2002 Anjou Villages Brissac, Cuvée J Beaujeau, Cabernet Franc, Château la Varière, Loire Valley, France, £7.99, Waitrose
This is the kind of gentle, almost shy and retiring red wine that can get lost in the flurry and bustle of a big tasting. But it stood out here – precisely because it was so fresh and bright and breezy. It's very dry, with a delightful mild flavour of raspberries, and its dryness is accented by a texture that is as cool and smooth as pebbles at the bottom of a stream.

❷ 2003 Viognier, Brampton, Coastal Region, South Africa, £7.99, Waitrose
Viognier is a warm-climate grape from France's Rhône Valley. When they get it right, it has a wonderfully exotic richness and sultry perfume. But it's not easy to grow and it's not easy to extract those flavours. The South Africans think the Viognier is ideal for them. Well, this is a good start. It hasn't got the kind of perfume to make your eyelids droop, but it has got lots of rich apricot fruit and a ginger/cinnamon spice.

❸ 2002 Gewurztraminer, Alsace, France, £6.99, Tesco
Gewurztraminer is famously aromatic. In fact it's probably the most aromatic variety of all when it really lets rip. This is a restrained example, not massively fragrant, but it still has a delightful rose petal smell. It tastes of honey and lychees, which might sound a bit cloying, but there's a refreshing streak of minerals and acidity that keeps the balance just right.

❹ 2003 Pinot Noir, Montana, New Zealand, £6.99, Waitrose
Montana have set out to produce the best affordable Pinot Noir in the world. They seem to control about half of all the Pinot plantings in New Zealand, so they might manage it. Certainly this 2003 has lovely plum and red cherry fruit, a hint of allspice and rather a beguiling perfume. I'd say they're on the right track.

For more wine recommendations see Oz Clarke's Wine Style Guide, pages 88–96

French classics

WHITE

Bourgogne Chardonnay, Alex Gambal (page 26)

Chablis, Tesco Finest (page 56)

Mâcon-Villages, Cave de Prissé (page 38)

Meursault, 1er Cru Les Perrières, J-M Gaunoux (page 21)

Meursault, Tesco Finest (page 54)

RED

Claret, Patrice Calvet (page 76)

Côtes de Castillon, Seigneurs d'Aiguilhe (page 52)

St-Emilion, Ch. La Rose Larmande (page 64)

St-Emilion, Yvon Mau (page 62)

SWEET

Sauternes, Yvon Mau (page 80)

Sauternes, Ch. Guiraud (page 80)

❺ **2002 Pinot Noir Reserve,** Las Brisas, Leyda, Chile, £8.99, Sainsbury's

Talking of places that are determined to excel at Pinot Noir, Chile has some cool coastal valleys with people just as determined as the New Zealanders. This is a serious wine – less perfume than the Montana above, but with a real Burgundian earthiness and strong ripe fruit. From a brand new region. Keep up the good work.

❻ **2002 Old Vines Garnacha, Campaneo,** Campo de Borja, Aragon, Spain, £5.99, Sainsbury's

There are an awful lot of old vines in the byways of Spanish wine that have just been sitting there for generations waiting for someone to put them to good use. The word is out, luckily, and winemakers are cooing over the quality of these long-neglected jewels that pulsate with rich blackberry and strawberry fruit yet have enough herbs and tannin to satisfy even the most serious-minded drinker.

❼ **2002 Viognier, Paul Mas,** Vin de Pays d'Oc, Languedoc-Roussillon, France, £5.52, Asda

Paul Mas are a family of grapegrowers who have recently got involved in making the wine rather than just selling the fruit – and they're doing very well. This Viognier is a delight, with a come-hither waft of rose petal fragrance and a gentle, mellow flavour of apricots that is just about as lush as you'd want and still be able to polish off the bottle.

❽ **1999 Rioja Reserva, Viña Mara,** Bodegas Berberana, Spain, £7.99, Tesco

Here's another Rioja (see the panel on page 58 for others) that shows it's worth spending a pound or two more for the real thing. This is a good, full, dry style, with delicate strawberry fruit, a touch of spice, and a bit of crème fraîche sour-edged softness that is very attractive.

uncork!

Bronze Medal

Gold Medal

Barton & Guestier®

— DEPUIS 1725 —

Purveyors of Joie de Vivre since 1725.

Supermarket selection

❾ 2001 Syrah, Marques de Griñon, Dominio de Valdepusa, Spain, £14.99, Waitrose

If Rioja doesn't tempt you, this couldn't be a more different Spanish style. No restraint, nothing low-key, just a power-packed full-on blast of rich, almost overripe plum and prune fruit, soaked in Fowlers Black Treacle and just barely freshened up with an attractive stewed vegetables depth. It's powerful and aggressive. It's also impressive and adds yet another facet to the rapidly changing face of Spain.

❿ 2003 Shiraz, Sainsbury's Classic Barossa, St Hallett, Australia, £6.99, Sainsbury's

The Barossa Valley is famous for making blockbuster Shirazes that knock you back into your chair with their power. Luckily there's another type too – particularly at the more affordable price level – and this is a good example. It's very dry, with good ripe black fruit balanced nicely by refreshing acidity. Certainly not a blockbuster and all the better for it.

⑪ 2002 St-Emilion, Yvon Mau, Bordeaux, France, £8.53, Tesco

This is good. St-Emilion is probably Bordeaux's most famous region, and it certainly has a number of Bordeaux's most over-priced properties within its borders. But it does make lovely wine – the trick is to try to locate examples that aren't a silly price. Well, let's have more like this one: typically dry – red Bordeaux should always be dry – with a nice oak richness rather like Ovaltine or Nesquik, good, lean, nutty fruit and just a nip of appetizing Bordeaux tannin.

> *'…red Bordeaux should always be dry – with a nice oak richness rather like Ovaltine'*

⑫ 2003 Pinotage, Diemersfontein, Wellington, South Africa, £6.99, Waitrose

This is a wine I went batty about on its first release. It's lost a bit of its otherworldly brilliance, but is still some mouthful – rich black fruit, ripe as anything but heavily overlaid with the toasted nut and coffee-chocolate flavour of aging in expensive new oak barrels. I'd say lay off the barrels a bit, save some money, because the fruit doesn't need any help.

⑬ 2003 Bordeaux Rosé, Domaine de Sours, France, £5.49, Sainsbury's

I'm always pleased when a rosé scores well, because it's such a delightful wine style, but people can get a bit sniffy about it. No need to here – 2003 was a very hot year and de Sours has made a deep, ripe, blazing pink wine whose soft strawberry fruit and fat texture tell you the sun shone long and hard on this vineyard.

---

⑭ 1999 Chianti Classico Riserva, Ampelos, Tuscany, Italy,
🍷 £6.99, Tesco

Chianti is not supposed to be a 'juicy Lucy' easy-come-easy-go kind of wine. It's supposed to have a bit of bite, some nervous acidity, some aggression to it. That's what the local Tuscan food demands. And this would go very well with a great slab of Florentine beefsteak, because it's lean and dry, its fruit is almost leafy and the flavour more of tomato than cherry or plum, with the rough scent of hillside herbs kicking in.

---

⑮ Tinta Miúda-Cabernet Sauvignon, DFJ Vinhos,
🍷 Estremadura, Portugal, £5.79, Budgens

Portugal proving once again that when it comes to original red wine flavours at an affordable price, they're hard to beat. This isn't quite as rich as some of DFJ's wines but has a good full round flavour like cherry fruit cake and a definite streak of leafy blackcurrant from the Cabernet Sauvignon.

---

⑯ 2001 Shiraz, Banwell Farm, St Hallett Wines, Barossa
🍷 Valley, South Australia, £8.99, Marks & Spencer

Pretty powerful Barossa Shiraz. 2001 was a vintage that produced some fairly chunky wines in South Australia and this shows in the slightly OTT style, where dried fruit, creamy toffee and an array of kitchen spices like allspice and coriander seed all throw themselves into the melting pot and no one's quite decided yet who'll come out on top.

---

⑰ 2003 Pinot Gris, Villa Maria, East Coast, New Zealand,
♀ £6.99, Waitrose

They're talking of Pinot Gris being the Next Big Thing in New Zealand. Well, I'm not sure about that, but they are producing some nice stuff, and this has a very pleasant, soft goldengage and loft apple flavour, just touched by icing sugar and straightened up with fresh acidity.

---

⑱ 1998 Rioja Reserva,Viña Caña, Spain, £6.99, Somerfield

🍷 Attractive, mature Rioja isn't that easy to find on the High Street. But this is six years old and will last another six if you want it to. 1998 was a fairly lean vintage and that shows in the wine's dry texture, but the strawberry fruit's there, and the coating of buttery custard from 20 months' aging in barrel calms down the streaks of mineral acidity darting through the wine.

Portugal

WHITE
Vinho Verde, Quinta de
Simaens (page 64)

RED
Manta Preta, DFJ Vinhos (page
64)
Portada, DFJ Vinhos (page 43)
Tinta Miúda-Cabernet
Sauvignon, DFJ Vinhos (page
63)
Touriga Nacional, Tesco (page
58)

**⓳ 2001 St-Emilion, Château
♦ La Rose Larmande,**
Bordeaux, France, £7.98, Asda
Good, serious St-Emilion,
maybe even a little stern
just now – it could use a
couple more years' aging –
but this is attractively
earthy, the red plum fruit is
soft and there's a definite
splash of the glycerine
texture and buttercream
mellowness that marks out
St-Emilion from the tougher
areas of Bordeaux.

**⓴ 2003 Gewürztraminer, Sierra Los Andes, Viña Carmen,
♀ Curicó, Chile, £5.99, Marks & Spencer**
I couldn't resist putting this in. After a hard day tasting
hundreds of dry reds and whites, this delightful, scented
crowd-pleaser turns up smelling of rose petals and melon,
and tasting of kiwi fruit and ripe pink grapefruit.

**㉑ 2001 Manta Preta, DFJ Vinhos, Estremadura,
♦ Portugal, £5.99, Waitrose**
This is one of the upmarket wines made by Portuguese
crowd-pleasers DFJ and their winemaker José Neiva. It's
packed with rich chocolate and oozing with super-ripe
damson and blackberry fruit. As a general rule, if you see the
words DFJ on an otherwise incomprehensible Portuguese red
label, it'll be good grog.

**㉒ 2002 Bonarda, Alamos, Catena Zapata, Mendoza,
♦ Argentina, £5.49, Booths**
Bonarda is a late-ripening Italian grape that is grown all over
the really hot parts of Argentina because it keeps its fresh
acidity however much sun it gets. And it isn't sexy – yet – so
the price is fair, but with its amazing wild strawberry taste and
taut acidity it can't be long before it becomes fashionable.

**㉓ 2003 Vinho Verde, Quinta de Simaens, Portugal,
♀ £5.49, Waitrose**
You hardly ever see real Vinho Verde in this country, and one
taste of this thrillingly aggressive wine could tell you precisely
why. But be brave, why don't you? You'll never have tasted a
white quite like this: punishingly dry, with the acidity of pure
lemon juice and a minerality like licking the lava off the slope
of an active volcano.

For the largest
choice of quality
Portuguese wines,
there's only
one place to go.

D&F
WINE SHIPPERS

Economy class

Last year our Economy class was based on wines at £3.99 and less. But the £4.99 price point has become such a battleground for wines, with many supermarkets demanding that wines can be sold for less than a fiver – regardless of whether it lets the producer make any profit – that we thought we'd give £4.99 its own section (or 'around a fiver', since prices sometimes rise a touch between me writing the notes and the book coming out). And we found that there is plenty of very tasty stuff for a fiver, as well as a lot of wine that has been stretched to breaking point to try to make this price point. Follow our recommendations for real 'five quid flavour'.

❶ 2003 Carmenère, Casillero del Diablo, Concha y Toro, Rapel Valley, Chile, £4.99, Sainsbury's

This is superb wine for £4.99. It's made by the mighty Concha y Toro company, and you're going to see several of their wines elsewhere in this guide. Chile's lucky to have such a quality-conscious major player, because the whole country is put on its mettle. Indeed Chile has made a quantum leap in quality below £5 in the past year, and for really tasty reds at this price, is, frankly, unbeatable. This shows why. Deep, powerful stuff, a mix of the savoury brilliance of an old-fashioned (i.e. my mum's) beef stew combined with black plums, black smoke, soy sauce and coffee. Dark and forbidding at first, it opens up in the glass to display memorable flavours for £4.99.

❷ 2002 Carmenère, Misiones de Rengo, Rapel Valley, Chile, £4.99, Somerfield

Carmenère again – it's a world-class grape, and only Chile has it – but this time it's from the ambitious Misiones de Rengo operation, but their approach is the same: toasty oak to give an exotic smoky quality, followed by rich, black-as-night fruit and savoury black chocolate, with the addition of what could be the scented blossom of a pepper tree.

❸ 2003 Chenin Blanc Reserve, Ken Forrester, Stellenbosch, South Africa, £4.99, Tesco

Ken Forrester is an artist of South Africa's Chenin grape – although don't plan an early morning meeting if you're having dinner with him the night before. He seeks out old plantations of Chenin – South Africa's most widely planted grape – and produces a variety of wines in a variety of styles. This is modern – fresh and balanced – but the acidity is contained in delightful greengage and Bramley apple fruit, ripe yet always acidic, and helped along by a streak of mineral dust.

ROSEMOUNT
ESTATE

Surround yourself in flavour

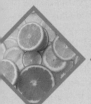

Rosemount
Melon Creek White
Chardonnay, Verdelho,
Sauvignon Blanc

A fruity and fresh wine
with citrus and zesty flavours.
Perfect as an aperitif or with
salads, chicken or Asian dishes.

Rosemount
Melon Creek Red
Shiraz, Mataro, Grenache

A soft and approachable wine
with berry and plum flavours
and a hint of spice and
well balanced oak. Ideal to
drink on its own or with lamb
or pasta dishes.

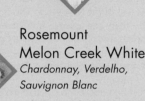

Exclusive to Asda RRP £4.98

R O S E M O U N T

❹ 2002 Semillon, Mountain Vines, Cyprus, £4.29, Co-op

🍷 Right – hold your breath everyone. This outstanding wine is from Cyprus. It may be the only outstanding white wine the island produces, but I cannot think of a classier, more delicious white at this price from anywhere in Europe! And if we all buy it, other Cypriot producers might be encouraged to make more effort. It's a beautifully round, soft, balanced Semillon with refreshing lemon acidity cutting across juicy nectarine fruit and custard cream oak. You'd be hard-pressed to get this quality in Semillon's homeland, Bordeaux, for less than ten quid.

❺ 2002 Pinot Grigio, The Boulders, California, USA, £4.99, Co-op

🍷 Most budget-priced Californian wine tastes flat and sweet and you can't finish the bottle. But the Co-op has taken a proactive line and found a producer who'll create good flavours at a fair price – just like the rest of the New World. This is bit like a Sauvignon in style – leafy and appley – but there's also a nice flavour of white peach, and it's very fresh for a Californian wine.

❻ 2002 Minervois, Languedoc-Roussillon, France, £4.99, Sainsbury's

🍷 Minervois at its best is supposed to smell of violets – and this one does! Not only violets but something that reminds me – I don't know how – of pink talcum powder. However, take a slug and this is proper red wine – burly, a bit tannic, but deep and ripe and bursting with the flavours of black cherries and plums.

❼ 2000 Altozano, Tempranillo-Merlot, Vino de la Tierra de Castilla, Spain, £4.99, Somerfield

🍷 Nice wine. Reminds me of a good Rioja, but at a significantly lower price. Well, that'll be the Tempranillo – Rioja's grape – and the attractive dry savoury cream, the mix of raisin and strawberry fruit and the hint of mint and pepper scent is exactly what you'd expect the Tempranillo to offer.

❽ 2003 Catarratto, Aramonte, Firriato, Sicily, Italy, £4.99, Marks & Spencer

🍷 Sicily is becoming one of the hotbeds of innovation in Italy after generations of slumber. Catarratto is a grape that used to be made into Marsala. What a waste. It's much better employed creating a bright soft white like this, smelling of peach talc and wild flowers, and tasting of spice and green melon fresh.

❾ 2002 Petite Sirah, The Boulders, California, USA, £4.99, Co-op

🍷 Another example of the Co-op being one of the few multiples who know how to coax good affordable wine out of the

Golden State. This is a little severe, but that's the character of the grape. It's a big, rough, unsubtle bruiser, but it rewards you with lots of clunky stewy plum skins and berries fruit to face down the tannin and the acidity.

⓿ 2003 Chardonnay-Viognier, Castel, Vin de Pays d'Oc, Languedoc-Roussillon, France, £4.99, Sainsbury's
Sometimes southern French Chardonnay a bit bland, and it really appreciates a slug of sexy Viognier. This example works well: refreshing lean Chardonnay given a floral scent and a pear flesh juiciness by the Viognier.

❶ 2002 Chardonnay, Vin de Pays d'Oc, Domaine Ste Agathe, Languedoc-Roussillon, France, £4.99, Somerfield
Of course, if you don't overcrop Chardonnay, you can make lovely stuff in France's south. This one's full, gentle, with some glycerine softness and nutty depth from oak barrel aging. Nice.

❷ 2003 Chardonnay, Vin de Pays d'Oc, Gold Label, Languedoc-Roussillon, France, £4.99, Marks & Spencer
Another good example of a southern French Chardonnay. This has soft melon fruit with a sliver of peach richness, a little warm dusty honey and a sprinkling of mild spice.

❸ 2003 Pinotage, Helderberg Winery, Stellenbosch, South Africa, £4.99, Budgens
You're going to love this or loathe it: Pinotage is a grape that takes no prisoners. It is incredibly smoky, has a rich mulberry fruit and a sweet heart of toasted marshmallows, which is needed to stand up to the rock-like rasp of the tannins. If you like the sound of it, this wine is for you.

❹ 2002 Muscadet Sèvre et Maine sur lie, Château de la Mouchetiere, Loire Valley, France, £4.99, Budgens
This reminds me of why Muscadet used to be such a delightful and popular summer drink. It has a bright appley fruit, a soft cream and nut yeastiness from spending time on the yeast lees (that's what 'sur lie' means) and is just a very pleasant summer white. That's all it ever set out to be.

❺ 2003 Chardonnay, Burra Brook, Lindemans, South Eastern Australia, £4.99, Marks & Spencer
This reminds me of the Lindemans Bin 65 of the old days, when it was probably the best commercial Chardonnay in the world. There's a bit more competition now, and the current Bin 65 is less good and more expensive, but this has a lovely warm smell of smoky roast nuts and a soft, easygoing fruit of melon, peach and banana. Very easy to drink glass after glass.

16 **2003 Riesling, Sainsbury's Australian,** **Knappstein, £4.99, Sainsbury's**
I almost said this is the perfect introduction to Australian Riesling. Well, yes it is, with its lemon blossom scent and soft but dry apple and lemon zest fruit. But it's really good in its own right. So, beginner or old-timer – don't fail to try this.

---

17 **2002 Zinfandel Reserve,** **San Joaquin Valley, California, USA, £4.99, Tesco**
The Californians think of Zinfandel as their own grape variety. Other places do grow it, but certainly California has defined the style – a rich groggy stew of plums, dates and figs, often laced with tobacco. This is a tad sweet for me, but the Zin flavour is spot on.

---

18 **2002 Shiraz, First Flight Reserve,** **South Eastern Australia, £4.99, Somerfield**
This is a pretty powerful mouthful, not subtle, but full of flavour – black chocolate and roasted nuts and plums – and if it is a little rough-edged, I'm not complaining.

---

19 **2003 Chilean Sauvignon Blanc Reserve,** **Viña San Pedro, Central Valley, Chile, £4.44, Asda**
We think of Chile as basically a red wine country, but they make loads of whites, and the big San Pedro outfit has always made good Sauvignon. This is really snappy, leafy, aggressive – ripe and acidic all at the same time – just as Sauvignon should be.

Everyday drinking

You really do get a lot more for your money when you trade up to £3.99 from £2.99. And you definitely get a wider range of countries and grape varieties. France, for instance, struggles at £2.99, but has more decent stuff at £3.99 than any other producer.

1 **2002 Fitou, Cuvée Rocher d'Embrée,** **Les Producteurs du Mont Tauch, Languedoc-Roussillon, France, £3.99, Somerfield**
Wherever you see 'Les Producteurs du Mont Tauch' in the small print on the label, you know you're going to get really characterful wine at a very fair price. They're the big co-op in the Corbières hills, and Fitou is their speciality. This dry, tasty red has a fabulous flavour of bay leaves and thyme to go with its raspberry. Southern French reds often taste of hillside herbs. This tastes as though they heaved the hillside into the vat.

For more wine recommendations see Oz Clarke's Wine Style Guide, pages 88–96

❷ 2002 Pinotage-Shiraz, Dumisani, Western Cape, South Africa, £3.64, Asda

Pinotage is a tricky grape to tame, so the canny producers don't try to tame it – they blend. What you get here is the powerful Pinotage flavours of burnt grilled steak and smoky mulberry, softened and calmed down by the mellow plum and raspberry flavours of the Shiraz.

❸ 2002 Coteaux du Languedoc, The Southern Collection, Les Coteaux du Pic, Languedoc-Roussillon, France, £3.79, Morrisons

Lots of character here from some of the best parts of the Languedoc. This tastes rich and ripe like a strawberry coulis, well balanced by acidity and a whiff of herbs and hardly any tannic surliness at all.

❹ 2002 Corbières, The Southern Collection, Les Vignerons de la Méditeranée, Languedoc-Roussillon, France, £3.49, Morrisons

Southern France again – what did I say about the value you can get in red wine from down there? This has a full, dry, red plum and red cherry fruit, streaked with minerals and seasoned with a fistful of bay leaves.

❺ 2002 Shiraz-Cabernet, First Flight, South Eastern Australia £3.99, Somerfield

Big, burly red for when the weather turns ugly. It has a solid, stewy black plums and chocolate flavour, but there are toasted nuts, too, and a bit of tannic attack. It tastes like proper wine rather than sugary grape juice like so many cheap Aussies.

❻ 2003 Cuvée Fleur Rosé, Vin de Pays de l'Herault, Languedoc-Roussillon, France, £3.49, Waitrose

This is about as fresh as a rosé can get – the pale pink colour opening out to a bright dry flavour of strawberries and Cox's Orange Pippin apples. Good value too.

❼ 2003 Mourvèdre-Shiraz, Tortoiseshell Bay, Casella Wines, South Eastern Australia, £3.99, Somerfield

Quite serious and quite restrained in style, but this has good black plum fruit balanced by fresh acidity, and a nice touch of chocolate depth.

❽ Valdepeñas Oak-aged Tempranillo, Félix Solís, Spain, £3.79 Co-op

Reds from central Spain can sometimes taste a bit baked. Well this certainly has very full-blown loganberry and strawberry

Southern French reds

ROSÉ

fruit, but it also has a stony dryness on one side and a soft toffee spice on the other, which makes for a well-balanced glass of grog.

❾ **Shiraz-Petit Verdot, Ransome's Vale,** Australia, £3.99 Aldi

Though Shiraz comes first on the label, it's the Petit Verdot here which gives the quality and the depth; this is serious red wine at this price. Dark, a little of that drying rasp that Bordeaux has, but far more of the deep black plum and blackberry which makes Petit Verdot such a good grape in Australia.

❿ **Old Vine Shiraz, Evolution,** Western Australia, £3.99, Aldi

Good, sturdy stuff packed with juicy fruit and real richness from ripe grapes. It's big and soft in style and with a strong blackberry flavour it's a bit like a blackberry cake in character – except that I've never heard of anyone making a blackberry cake.

⓫ **2003 Vin de Pays du Gers, Vignoble de Gascogne,** South-West France, £3.49, Marks & Spencer

This is one of the High Street's most reliable gluggers if you like your wine sharp and tangy. It comes from the far south-west of France and has a sharp flavour of lemon and green apples and blackcurrant leaves and a dryness like rain-washed pebbles.

12 2002 Chilean Chardonnay, Viña Morandé, Central Valley, £4.03, Somerfield

They used to make lots of tropical-tasting Chardonnay in the New World, full of figgy flavours, peaches, pineapple and a good wallop of oak. Well, there aren't many examples left, but this is a pretty good New World old-timer.

13 2002 Chilean Cabernet Sauvignon, Viña Cornellana, Rapel Valley, Chile, £4.03, Somerfield

Not subtle, but lots of flavour – gentle blackcurrant fruit and even a little blackcurrant syrup richness, with the cool earth of the vineyards tugging gently on the easy fruit.

14 2003 Côtes du Ventoux, La Rectorie, Rhône Valley, France, £3.99, Waitrose

They've had an Aussie winemaker in here helping to bring out the fruit flavours in the grapes, and it's paid off. This has very attractive strawberry-red fruit, but it's quite solid – as it needs to be to cope with the noticeable Rhône Valley tannins.

Southern French whites

Chardonnay, Les Argelières, Vin de Pays (page 38)
Chardonnay, Vin de Pays, Marks & Spencer (page 69)
Chardonnay, Vin de Pays, Somerfield (page 69)
Chardonnay-Viognier, Castel, Vin de Pays (page 69)
Chardonnay-Viognier, La Chasse du Pape, Vin de Pays (page 39)
Jurançon Sec, Dom. Castera (page 32)
Limoux Chardonnay, Ch. Rive-Blanques (page 28)
Limoux Chardonnay, Sieur d'Arques (page 33)
Vin de Pays du Gers, Marks & Spencer (page 72)
le Soula, Gauby, Vin de Pays (page 27)
Viognier, Paul Mas, Vin de Pays (page 60)

SPARKLING
Crémant de Limoux (page 78)
Gaillac, Mauzac Nature, Dom. des Tres Cantous (page 46)

SWEET
Muscat de Frontignan, Dom. d'Arain (page 81)

15 2002 Fitou, The Southern Collection, Les Producteurs du Mont Tauch, Languedoc-Roussillon, France, £4.29, Morrisons

Good soft but dry red with lots of attractive raspberry fruit and a serious dose of bayleaf and thyme.

16 2002 Minervois, The Southern Collection, Les Vignerons Catalans, Languedoc-Roussillon, France, £3.99, Morrisons

Minervois can have a seductive violet scent. This example, however, is altogether manly and has a rather rough, savoury smell, but this blends in pretty well with the solid, ripe red plum fruit at the heart of the wine.

Supermarket selection

⑰ Viognier, California, £3.99, Tesco
♀ This is pretty good. So it should be: the conditions in much of
California are ideal for Viognier. But decent Californian wine
at this price is a real rarity and this is most attractive, soft,
creamy and with a gentle peach and pear flesh fruit.

⑱ 2003 House Wine, Vin de Pays du Comté Tolosan,
♥ **Plaimont, South-West France, £3.29, Marks & Spencer**
Delightful light red, unassuming, uncomplicated and very
pleasant to drink, with its leafy freshness, juicy red plum fruit
and vineyard earthiness.

⑲ Fitou, Les Caves de Mont Tauch, Languedoc-Roussillon,
♥ **France, £3.52, Asda**
Fairly light for a Fitou and with a little citrous acidity –
probably from 2002 vintage fruit that wasn't fully ripe – but
it's very refreshing, dry, plummy and scented with bay leaf.

⑳ 2003 Cariñena, Gran Tempranillo, Vitivinicola de Longares,
♥ **Spain, £3.29, Sainsbury's**
It's very hot in Cariñena, one of Spain's ancient winelands
that we haven't seen much of until recently. So the grapes get
baked, but so long as you like the flavour of sun-dried
tomatoes and stewed cranberries, you should like this.

㉑ 2002 Torrontes-Chardonnay, La Riojana, Famatina Valley,
♀ **Argentina, £3.79, Co-op**
This isn't going to be everyone's cup of tea, but it does have
loads of character. It's got an attractive floral scent, but that is
quickly swamped by a cavalcade of pineapple, ginger, green
melon and boiled lemon peel. Not for everyone, but I like it.

㉒ 2002 Argentinian Malbec, La Riojana, Famatina Valley,
♥ **Argentina, £3.74, Asda**
It's nice to find a cheery red that has a juicy, fat, sun-soaked
character without tasting baked and exhausted. This isn't
perfumed – Malbec sometimes is – but it's got lots of chunky
red plum fruit and a warm, dusty aftertaste. Which is fitting:
the Famatina Valley is one of the dustiest vineyard regions
I've ever visited.

㉓ 2003 Argentine Sangiovese, La Agricola/Zuccardi,
♥ **Mendoza, Argentina, £3.99, Somerfield**
Sangiovese is the grape of Italy's Chianti – but it never tasted
like this! This has such a fruity smell it's like bananas and
strawberries mashed with cream and eaten in a sandwich.
When you drink it, the wine is a bit rougher than that, but the
bananas and strawberries linger just long enough.

Bargain basement

Things are getting tougher at the bargain basement end of wine. Last year we managed to find 20 decent drops. This year we searched just as hard and only came up with 14. But six of the top seven are from Chile, and if I could give one piece of advice to bargain hunters today, it is – head for Chile.

❶ 2003 Carmenère, Paso del Sol, Terramater, Central Valley, Chile, **£2.99,** Morrisons
Wonderful stuff and unbelievable value. Packed with rich, ripe blue and black fruit, seasoned with celery salt and pepper and perfumed with sandalwood – this is a triumph.

❷ Chilean Merlot, £2.99, Sainsbury's
Another superb Chilean crowd-pleaser, but in a gentler mode. Refreshing leafy acidity brightens up the easygoing, gluggable ripe red fruit, with a touch of soy sauce and pepper seasoning.

❸ Chilean Cabernet Sauvignon, Viña Las Cabras, Rapel Valley, **£2.99,** Sainsbury's
And more Chile. This is more powerful than the Merlot above, with a raw, self-confident surge of black chocolate and blackcurrant swirled with a little smoke and acidity, and a touch of appetizing bitterness. Bring out the barbie.

❹ 2003 Chilean Cabernet Sauvignon, Viña San Pedro, Central Valley, **£2.97,** Asda
Chile again? Yes. This is the giant San Pedro's version of Cabernet, smelling of coffee beans and blackcurrant leaf and tasting of plums and blackcurrant. Dry and appetizing.

❺ 2003 First Flight Australian Dry Red, South Eastern Australia, **£2.99,** Somerfield
Good, fresh, juicy Aussie red which even has a bit of perfume to brighten up the ripe jammy flavours of plum and cherry.

❻ 2003 Chilean Chardonnay, Viña San Pedro, Central Valley, **£2.97,** Asda
Chile, yes, but it's white this time – a very pleasant and surprisingly leafy dry white with soft peach and green apple fruit making a very nice drink for less than three quid.

❼ 2003 Chilean Sauvignon Blanc, Viña San Pedro, Central Valley, **£2.97,** Asda
This is about as fresh as you're going to get from Chile – it

even has an attractive hint of spritz to make it fresher still, though with this tangy lemon leaf and green apple flavour and the hint of minty perfume, it hardly needs to be fresher.

❽ 2002 Claret, Patrice Calvet, Bordeaux, France, £2.99, Aldi

Aldi have some rather good Bordeaux reds, both expensive and cheap. This is almost revolutionary – a screwcap on a red wine from stuffy old Bordeaux. Well, it works. The wine has kept a bit of perfume and has some dark plummy fruit to go with the typical Bordeaux earthiness.

❾ Argentinian Red Wine, La Riojana, Famatina Valley, £2.56, Asda

A wine from the excellent but underrated Bonarda grape that's thick with gutsy ripe red fruit and scented with strawberry. If that makes it sound slightly subtle, it isn't – but it's a proper tasty gobful of red.

❿ 2002 Chardonnay, Budavar, Hungary, £2.49, Aldi

You can't beat this at the price. It's a bit earthy – but so is lots of Chablis for three times the money – but this wine makes up for it with attractive spicy pear and banana fruit and a tug of refreshing acidity. Hungary does this style of wine really well.

⓫ 2003 Merlot, Paso del Sol, Terramater, Central Valley, Chile, £2.99, Morrisons

Pleasantly plummy basic Merlot, with quite a serious earthy undertow and a touch of tannin, but nice fresh red plum fruit making it easy to drink

⓬ Argentinian White Wine, La Riojana, Famatina Valley, £2.59, Asda

This is not your average dry, flat £2.59 white. They've thrown in some interesting Argentine grape varieties and the result is a very fresh white full of pineapple and melon fruit, with a fairly powerful perfume of Rose's lime juice cordial.

⓭ Badgers Creek, South Eastern Australia, £2.99, Aldi

There's not much decent Aussie white any more at the lower price points, so this is a pleasant surprise: good melon and apple fruit, a touch of peachy spice – and not too *sweet*.

⓮ 2002 Corbières, Vignerons de la Méditerranée, Languedoc-Roussillon, France, £2.99, Sainsbury's

Not massively ripe – 2002 was a bit cold – but if you don't mind the lean style, this has quite an attractive herb scent to go with the cool-vintage red fruit.

Supermarket sparklers

There are some good supermarket Champagnes around this year, and it's encouraging to see how even the big-volume stores like Tesco and Sainsbury's put some pretty decent bubbles into their own labels. But who's that sitting on top of the pile? England. We've been saying for years that England has the potential to make wine as good as Champagne. Well, now it's happening.

❶ 2000 Bloomsbury Cuvée Merret Brut, Ridgeview Estate, West Sussex, England, £14.99, Waitrose
The chalky downland soils of much of southern England are exactly the same as the best soils in Champagne – which is only a couple of hours drive in the car from Calais. Global warming, careful vineyard management and brilliant winemaking have produced this gorgeous, rich yet dry fizz, smelling like every Ovaltine and Horlicks that sent you to bed as a kid but cut through with apple peel and lemon acidity and a torrent of foam that is inspiring and delicious.

❷ 1996 Champagne Brut, P & C Heidsieck, £19.99, Waitrose
Aren't any of you buying this, or what? This is the third year that the 1996 vintage has been offered by Waitrose. Well that's fine by me, because each year the wine gets softer and fuller. 1996 is a great year for Champagne, but the acidity *is* high, so this won't peak for another 5 years. Even so, it's impressive stuff now, but a little haughty and reserved, with strong green apple and lemon acidity but a gradually deepening nut and raisin richness to balance the wine.

❸ NV Champagne Brut, Blanc de Noirs, £13.99, Sainsbury's
Sainsbury's make something of a speciality of this. Blanc de Noirs Champagne is made from black grapes and should be richer and fatter than white-grape champagne. Spot on. This is rich and full of nutty, yeasty depth, a bit of almost strawberry fruit and refreshing acidity.

❹ NV Champagne Brut, Premier Cru, Prince William, Union Champagne, £13.99, Somerfield
Somerfield get their Prince William fizz from one of the best villages in Champagne – which explains why it's one of the most consistently enjoyable own-label Champagnes on the High Street: ripe, creamy, with a lovely foaming bubble and a nice acidity to nip the tip of your tongue.

For more wine recommendations see Oz Clarke's Wine Style Guide, pages 88–96

❺ NV Champagne Blanc de Blancs, France, £16.99, Tesco
Champagne made solely from the Chardonnay grape, but
from two separate districts. The majority comes from the great
swathe of limestone slopes that makes up the Côtes des
Blancs, but they've also added in some fruit from the village of
Sézanne, further south, which is famous for the honeyed
softness of its fruit and the fluffy freshness of its foam.

**❻ Sparkling Shiraz, Banrock Station, Australia,
£7.99, Somerfield**
Ha ha – happy juice. Sometimes in the middle of a hard wine
tasting you begin to wonder if you're ever going to have any
fun ever again. And then this turns up. A great big blast of all
the things you're not supposed to find in fizz. It's red for a
start, and it's got so much ripe fruit flavour – fabulous
blackcurrant and plums, chocolate, spice and treacle – that
you think, wow, really good Shiraz. Which is just what it is.
Really good Shiraz with bubbles in it. *Widely available.*

**❼ Crémant de Limoux Brut, Cuvée Royale, Languedoc-
Roussillon, France, £6.99, Waitrose**
There was a time, not that long ago, when Limoux fizz was
really trendy and everyone said it was just as good as
Champagne. Well, it's entirely likely they started making
sparkling wine in these lovely, lonesome hills of France's far
south-west before they started in Champagne. But it's always
tasted different. The Mauzac grape grows nowhere else, and
gives a zingy, in-yer-face green apple fruit to the wine, which
is softened just a little by Chenin and Chardonnay, but
remains an orchard apple bubbly.

❽ Sparkling White Burgundy, France, £7.99, Waitrose
They use Burgundy grape varieties to make wine in
Champagne. They use the Champagne method to make their
wines sparkle in Burgundy. The result is a very refreshing,
austere fruit flavour rather like a Chablis, a lovely foaming
bubble that is just like Champagne – and a price that is a lot
cheaper than any decent Champagne *I've* found.

❾ 1998 Vintage Cava, Spain, £6.99, Somerfield
I know this is a bit expensive for Cava, but this is pretty
interesting stuff. OK, I know you don't normally buy Cava for
'interesting' flavours – often you're trying to avoid anything
too interesting – just bubbles, nice 'n' cold. But this *is*
interesting. It's six years old for a start – that's almost
unheard of for a Cava – and the flavour is deep and ripe, with
a lemon zest scent keeping it very fresh, yet a full mellow
creaminess letting you know this ain't no spring chicken.

🔟 1998 Champagne Grand Cru, De St-Gall,
£19.99, Marks & Spencer

I don't know if any of you feel like buying a bottle or two of fizz and putting it under the stairs for a few years. If so, this is the one. Marks & Sparks fizz is always good and this one will age brilliantly and be at its best five years from now. Even at the moment it's got enough creamy softness to combat the apple skin acidity, enough nutty depth to bring a smile to your lips – but they won't be able to wipe that smile from your face if you leave this wine a few years.

⓫ English Sparkling Brut, Rivaner-Reichensteiner, £7.99, Co-operative

If you want to dip your toe in the world of good old Blighty's bubbly, try this – appley, dry but gentle, and with an attractive but challenging cool streak of mineral dust. Other merchants may have a fizz called Chapel Down: it's made by the same people and will be similarly good.

⓬ NV Cava Rosé Brut, Seleccion Especial, Marqués de Monistrol, £6.49, Waitrose

Rather serious stuff. It's dry, for a start, and it's got a quite stern mineral streak, and the fruit is just verging on the 'past its best' – but fresh fruit isn't necessary for good fizz, and this all adds up to a satisfying, rather serious, glass of bubbly.

Fortified & sweet wines

We've made a particular effort to seek out supermarket sherries this year. Why? Firstly because the quality of own-label – thank goodness – is beginning to improve. And if the big retailers want to steer the sherry world out of its current tailspin, decent quality at a decent price wouldn't be a bad idea. Secondly, Gordon Ramsay's *Hell's Kitchen* was sponsored by Tio Pepe Dry Sherry. Sales went up by 25% as a result of the expletive-deleted series. If the quality's good, people will come back for a second taste. If it isn't they won't. Seems terribly simple to me.

① 1989 Vintage Port, Morgan Brothers, Portugal,
£30, Marks & Spencer [SWEET]

This is pretty serious stuff. Vintage Port *is* serious, and it *is* expensive. So you have to decide: do you want the vintage experience? If you do, here it is. A deep, dark wine, exploding with exotic scents, awash with the richness of blackberries and heavy black plums, but shot through with pepper and reined in by the palate-cleansing bitterness of tannin.

❷ 2001 Sauternes, Yvon Mau, Bordeaux, France, £11.99/half bottle, Tesco Finest [SWEET]

This isn't just a superior blend, it's actually a single château wine, bottled at the property, and seriously classy. Fine Sauternes has a luscious waxy fatness, and this lanolin and beeswax texture dominates the wine, but also lets us revel in the rich ripeness of pineapple and cling peaches in syrup.

❸ 1998 Late Bottled Vintage Port, Smith Woodhouse, Portugal, £8.49, Waitrose [SWEET]

Late bottled vintage port, when properly done, brings you a lot of the flavours of Vintage Port, but without the brute power and majestic depth. This has a deep rich blackberry syrup fruit sprinkled with pepper and swished with herbs. Almost vintage in personality, and at this price, 'almost' is rather good.

❹ 2002 Sauternes, Sainsbury's Classic Selection, Château Guiraud, Bordeaux, France, £7.99/half bottle [SWEET]

Classic Sauternes – not dense or hefty, but with a gentle butterscotch and crystallized pineapple richness and an intriguing mineral acidity which makes it perfect for drinking by itself or with fresh fruit.

❺ Aged Tawny Port (10 year old Tawny), Portugal, £10.99, Marks & Spencer [SWEET]

This wine has been stored in wooden barrels for at least 10 years. This would kill a table wine, but port is sweet and fortified with spirit to the extent that it's really rough and fearsome when young. But aging in barrels makes it softer and lighter and imparts a nutty richness – like really ripe hazelnuts or Brazil nuts – as well as raisin sweetness and the delicious gooiness of syrup.

❻ 2001 Riesling Eiswein, Ruppertsberger Linsenbusch, Winzerverein Hoheburg, Pfalz, Germany, £14.99/half bottle, Sainsbury's [SWEET]

I don't know how this marvellous oddball is going to fare at £14.99 a half. But it is fascinating wine so I hope Sainsbury's can sell it. Because the acidity is high it doesn't seem that rich and it has a fatness of melted butter and syrup, a strange mineral taste like putty and the whiff of hillside herbs.

❼ Extra Dry Fino Sherry, Sanchez Romate, Spain, £5.03, Tesco [DRY]

Tio Pepe is a fino sherry: this is a cheaper version – bone dry, nutty, rather yeasty in that curious blend of soft and creamy with wild and sour that you get if you bake your own bread.

❽ Manzanilla Pale Dry Sherry, Francisco Gonzalez Fernandez, Spain, £4.99, Sainsbury's [DRY]
Manzanilla sherry is just that bit lighter and drier than Fino. It comes from the sea coast and some people think it tastes a bit salty. Well, it's certainly savoury – that nuttiness and brioche yeastiness is very dry – and would go brilliantly with a plate of salted almonds as you sit by the sea and ponder dinner.

❾ Rich Cream Sherry, Solera Jerezana, Diego Romero, Spain, £6.49, Waitrose [SWEET]
This is the kind of sherry that many of us started on at childhood Christmas times – a sip of a sweet, sometimes sickly brew as the carol singers laboured through their tunes. Well, this is sweet, but it isn't sickly, and the rich syrup of raisins, sultanas and figs coats your mouth in a very soothing manner.

❿ Extra Dry Manzanilla Sherry, Williams & Humbert, Spain, £4.99, Marks & Spencer [DRY]
Deliciously savoury, bone dry, this manages to be austere at the same time as being surprisingly soft, and that freshly yeasted bread dough flavour lingers on your palate and demands that you think of a few nibbles to go with it.

⓫ Dry Amontillado Sherry, Solera Jerezana, Diego Romero, Spain, £6.49, Waitrose [DRY]
Amontillado is often thought of as a vaguely sweet, predictably boring wine. Well, real Amontillado is actually dry – but it does leave a unique rich flavour of hazelnuts and the caramel toffee that coats buttered brazils.

⓬ 2003 Sweet Surrender Pudding Wine, Breede River Valley, South Africa, £4.99/half bottle, Co-op [SWEET]
This is rather nice and could just about coax me into accepting an offer that perhaps I should refuse. It has a rich pineapple and melon fruit and a good dose of lemon acidity to warn me to just say no.

⓭ Muscat de Frontignan, Domaine d'Arain, Languedoc-Roussillon, France, £3.99/50 cl, Somerfield [SWEET]
If you want a really good slug of rich, viscous grapey syrup, all honeyed and lush and not a bit subtle, this is a bargain buy. In southern France they sometimes sip this ice-cold as an aperitif.

⓮ Fletcher's Fine Ruby Port, Portugal, £4.49, Aldi [SWEET]
You simply can't beat this one for value. For subtlety, for elegance, for complexity – sure you can beat it. But if port's supposed to be rich and powerful and slurped down to keep out the cold – this does the job.

Storing, serving, tasting

Wine is all about enjoyment, so don't let anyone make you anxious about opening, serving, tasting and storing it. Here are some tips to help you enjoy your wine all the more.

THE CORKSCREW

The first step in tasting any wine is to extract the cork. Look for a corkscrew with an open spiral and a comfortable handle. The Screwpull brand is far and away the best, with a high-quality open spiral. 'Waiter's friend' corkscrews – the type you see used in restaurants – are good too, once you get the knack.

Corkscrews with a solid core that looks like a giant woodscrew tend to mash up delicate corks or get stuck in tough ones. A simple non-levered screw can require a heroic effort. And try to avoid those 'butterfly' corkscrews with the twin lever arms and a bottle opener on the end; they tend to leave cork crumbs floating in the wine.

CORKS

Don't be a cork snob. The only requirements for the seal on a bottle of wine are that it should be hygienic, airtight, long-lasting and removable. Real cork is environmentally friendly, but is prone to shrinkage and infection, which can taint the wine. Synthetic closures modelled on the traditional cork are common in budget wines and are increasingly used by high-quality producers, as are screwcaps, or Stelvin closures.

THE WINE GLASS

The ideal wine glass is a fairly large tulip shape, made of fine, clear glass, with a slender stem. This shape helps to concentrate the aromas of the wine and to show off its colours and texture. For sparkling wine choose a tall, slender glass, as it helps the bubbles to last longer.

Look after your glasses carefully. Detergent residues or grease can affect the flavour of any wine and reduce the bubbliness of sparkling wine. Ideally, wash glasses in very hot water and don't use detergent at all. Rinse glasses thoroughly and allow them to air-dry. Store wine glasses upright to avoid trapping stale odours.

DECANTING

Transferring wine to a decanter brings it into contact with oxygen, which can open up the flavours. You don't need to do it ages before serving and you don't need a special decanter: a glass jug is just as good. And there's no reason why you shouldn't decant the wine to aerate it, then pour it back into its bottle to serve it.

Mature red wine is likely to contain sediment and needs careful handling. Stand the bottle upright for a day or two to let the sediment fall to the bottom. Open the wine carefully, and place a torch or candle beside the decanter. As you pour, stand so that you can see the light shining through the neck of the bottle. Pour the wine into the decanter in one

Riedel "O" is a dramatic new departure in stemware - the stemless Riedel glass. Riedel "O" offers a relaxed approach to wine-specific glasses, minimising breakage and storage problems.

For Riedel stockists, please contact Riedel Crystal UK on 01782 646105

email: info@riedelcrystal.co.uk
web: www.riedel.com

RIEDEL

THE WINE GLASS COMPANY

steady motion and stop when you see the sediment reaching the neck of the bottle.

TEMPERATURE

The temperature of wine has a bearing on its flavour. Heavy reds are happy at room temperature, but the lighter the wine the cooler it should be. Juicy, fruity young reds, such as wines from the Loire Valley, are refreshing served lightly chilled; I'd serve Burgundy and other Pinot Noir reds at cool larder temperature.

Chilling white wines makes them taste fresher, but also subdues flavours, so bear this in mind if you're splashing out on a top-quality white – don't keep it in the fridge too long. Sparkling wines, however, *must* be well chilled to avoid exploding corks and fountains of foam.

For quick chilling fill a bucket with ice and cold water, plus a few spoonfuls of salt if you're in a real hurry. This is much more effective than a fridge or ice on its own. If the wine is already cool a vacuum-walled cooler is ideal for maintaining the temperature.

KEEPING LEFTOVERS

Exposure to oxygen causes wine to deteriorate. It lasts fairly well if you just push the cork back in and stick the bottle in the fridge, but you can also buy a range of effective devices to help keep oxygen at bay. Vacuvin uses a rubber stopper and a vacuum pump to remove air from the bottle. Others inject inert gas into the bottle to shield the wine from the ravages of oxidation.

WINE STORAGE

The longer you keep a bottle of wine, the more important it is to store it with care. If you've got a cellar, lucky you. If not, look around for a nook – under the stairs, a built-in cupboard or a disused fireplace – that is cool, relatively dark and vibration-free, in which you can store the bottles on their sides to keep the corks moist (if a cork dries out it will let air in and spoil the wine).

Wine should be kept in a cool place – around 10–15°C/50–55°F – well away from central heating. It is even more important to avoid sudden temperature changes or extremes: a windowless garage or outhouse may be cool in summer but may freeze in winter. Exposure to light can very quickly ruin wine, but dark bottles go some way to protecting it from light.

How to taste wine

If you just knock your wine back like a cold beer, you'll be missing most of whatever flavour it has to offer. Take a bit of time to pay attention to what you're tasting and I guarantee you'll enjoy the wine more.

Read the label

There's no law that says you have to make life hard for yourself when tasting wine. So have a look at what you're drinking and read the notes on the back label if there is one. The label will tell you the vintage, the region and/or the grape variety, the producer and the alcohol level.

Look at the wine

Pour the wine into a glass so it is a third full and tilt it against a white background so you can enjoy the range of colours in the wine. Is it dark or light? Is it viscous or watery? As you gain experience the look of the wine will tell you one or two things about the age and the likely flavour and weight of the wine. As a wine ages, whites lose their springtime greenness and gather deeper, golden hues, whereas red wines trade the purple of youth for a paler brick red.

Swirl and sniff

Give the glass a vigorous swirl to wake up the aromas in the wine, stick your nose in and inhale gently. This is where you'll be hit by the amazing range of smells a wine can produce. Interpret them in any way that means something to you personally: it's only by reacting honestly to the taste and smell of a wine that you can build up a memory bank of flavours against which to judge future wines.

Take a sip

At last! It's time to drink the wine. So take a decent-sized slurp – enough to fill your mouth about a third full. The tongue can detect only very basic flavour elements: sweetness at the tip, acidity at the sides and bitterness at the back. The real business of tasting goes on in a cavity at the back of the mouth which is really part of the nose. The idea is to get the fumes from the wine to rise up into this nasal cavity. Note the toughness, acidity and sweetness of the wine then suck some air through the wine to help the flavours on their way. Gently 'chew' the wine and let it coat your tongue, teeth, cheeks and gums. Jot down a few notes as you form your opinion and then make the final decision... Do you like it or don't you?

Swallow or spit it out

If you are tasting a lot of wines, you will have to spit as you go if you want to remain upright and retain your judgement. Otherwise, go ahead and swallow and enjoy the lovely aftertaste of the wine.

WINE FAULTS

If you order wine in a restaurant and you find one of these faults you are entitled to a replacement. Many retailers will also replace a faulty bottle if you return it the day after you open it, with your receipt. Sometimes faults affect random bottles, others may ruin a whole case of wine.

- Cork taint – a horrible musty, mouldy smell indicates 'corked' wine, caused by a contaminated cork
- Volatile acidity – pronounced vinegary or acetone smells
- Oxidation – sherry-like smells are not appropriate in red and white wines
- Hydrogen sulphide – 'rotten eggs' smell.

WATCHPOINTS

- Sediment in red wines makes for a gritty, woody mouthful. To avoid this, either decant the wine or simply pour it gently, leaving the last few centilitres of wine in the bottle.
- White crystals, or tartrates, on the cork or at the bottom of bottles of white wine are both harmless and flavourless.
- Sticky bottle neck – if wine has seeped past the cork it probably hasn't been very well kept and air might have got in. This may mean oxidized wine.
- Excess sulphur dioxide is sometimes noticeable as a smell of a recently struck match; it should dissipate after a few minutes.

Wine style guide

When faced with a shelf – or a screen – packed with
different wines from around the world, where do you
start? Well, if you're after a particular flavour of wine, my
guide to wine styles will point you in the right direction.

RED WINES
Juicy, fruity reds

The definitive modern style for easygoing reds.
Tasty, refreshing and delicious with or without
food, they pack in loads of crunchy fruit while
minimizing the tough, gum-drying tannins that characterize
most traditional red wine styles. Beaujolais (made from the Gamay
grape) is the prototype, and Loire reds such as Chinon and Saumur
(made from Cabernet Franc) pack in the fresh raspberries. Italy's
Bardolino is light and refreshing. Nowadays, hi-tech producers all ov
the world are working the magic with a whole host of grape varietie
Carmenère and Merlot are always good bets, and Grenache/Garnach
and Tempranillo usually come up with the goods. Italian grapes like
Bonarda, Barbera and Sangiovese seem to double in succulence und
Argentina's blazing sun. And at around £5 even Cabernet Sauvignon
if it's from somewhere warm like Australia, South America, South
Africa or Spain – or a vin de pays Syrah from southern France, will
emphasize the fruit and hold back on the tannin.

- **2003 Bonarda-Sangiovese, Terra Organica,** Familia Zuccardi,
  Mendoza, Argentina, £4.99, Somerfield
- **2002 Grenache, Peter Lehmann,** Barossa, Australia, £5–6,
  Flagship Wines, Oddbins, Morrisons, Tesco, Unwins
- **2003 Campaneo, Garnacha Old Vine,** Campo de Borja,
  Bodegas Aragonesas, Aragón, Spain, £5.99, Sainsbury's
- **2002 Beaujolais, Jean François Garlon,** Burgundy, France, £7.4⁵
  Roger Harris
- **2002 Anjou Villages Brissac, Cuvée J Beaujeau,** Château La
  Varière, Loire Valley, France, £7.99, Waitrose

Silky, strawberryish reds

Here we're looking for some special qualities, specifically a
gorgeously smooth texture and a heavenly fragrance of
strawberries, raspberries or cherries. We're lookir
for soft, decadent, seductive wines. One
grape – Pinot Noir – and one region
Burgundy – stand out and prices are
high to astronomical. Good red

Burgundy is addictively hedonistic and all sorts of strange
decaying aromas start to hover around the strawberries as the
wine ages. Pinot Noirs from New Zealand, California, Oregon and,
increasingly, Australia come close, but they're expensive, too;
Chilean Pinots are far more affordable. You can get that strawberry
perfume (though not the silky texture) from other grapes in
Spain's Navarra or Rioja and up-coming regions like La Mancha and
Murcia. Southern Rhône blends can deliver if you look for fairly
light examples of Côtes du Rhône-Villages or Costières de Nîmes.

- **2003 Pinot Noir, Cono Sur**, Rapel Valley, Chile, around £5,
  Budgens, Majestic, Morrisons, Oddbins, Somerfield, Tesco,
  Unwins, Waitrose
- **2002 Lacrima di Morra d'Alba Rubico**, Marotti Campi, Marche,
  Italy, £7.99, Oddbins
- **2003 Pinot Noir, Ninth Island**, Tasmania, Australia, around £9,
  Connolly's, Waitrose, Noel Young
- **1997 Rioja Reserva, Finca Valpiedra**, Spain, £15.99,
  Oddbins
- **2002 Pinot Noir, Quartz Reef**, Central Otago, New
  Zealand, £17.95, Lay & Wheeler, New Zealand Wines Direct

Intense, blackcurranty reds

Firm, intense wines which often only reveal their softer
side with a bit of age; Cabernet Sauvignon is the grape,
on its own or blended with Merlot or other varieties.
Bordeaux is the classic region but there are far too
many overpriced underachievers there. And
Cabernet's image has changed. You can still
choose the austere, tannic style, in theory
aging to a heavenly cassis and cedar maturity,
but most of the world is taking a fruitier
blackcurrant-and-mint approach. Chile does the
fruity style par excellence. New Zealand can deliver Bordeaux-
like flavours, but in a faster-maturing wine. Australia often adds a
medicinal eucalyptus twist or a dollop of blackcurrant jam.
Argentina and South Africa are making their mark too.

- **2001 Villa Maria Reserve Merlot-Cabernet Sauvignon**,
  Hawkes Bay, New Zealand, £14.99, Wimbledon Wine Cellar
- **2000 Cabernet Sauvignon, Nativa, Carmen**, Maipo Valley,
  Chile, £7.99, Butlers Wine Cellar, Oddbins, Waitrose, Wright Wine
- **2001 Cabernet Sauvignon, High Trellis, d'Arenberg**, McLaren
  Vale, South Australia, £8.49, Booths, Flying Corkscrew, Oddbins
- **2000 Cabernet Sauvignon, Vergelegen**, Stellenbosch,
  South Africa, £13.99, Oddbins
- **1999 Terrazas Gran Cabernet Sauvignon**, Mendoza,
  Argentina, £19.50, S H Jones, Wimbledon Wine Cellar

Spicy, warm-hearted reds

Australian Shiraz is the epitome of this rumbustious, riproaring style:
dense, rich, chocolaty, sometimes with a twist of pepper, a whiff of
smoke, or a slap of leather. But it's not alone. There are southern
Italy's Primitivo and Nero d'Avola, California's Zinfandel,
Mexico's Petite Sirah, Argentina's Malbec, South Africa's
Pinotage, Toro from Spain and some magnificent Greek reds
In southern France the wines of the Languedoc often show
this kind of warmth, roughed up with hillside herbs. And if
you want your spice more serious, more smoky and minerally,
go for the classic wines of the northern Rhône Valley.

- 2003 **Nero d'Avola-Syrah,** Sicily, Italy, £4.99, Marks & Spencer
- 2002 **Les Grands Augustins, Tardieu-Laurent, Vin de Pays d'Oc,** Languedoc-Roussillon, France, £6.99, Raeburn Fine Wines
- 2002 **Shiraz, Wolfkloof,** Robertson, South Africa, £8.70, Anthony Byrne
- 2001 **Shiraz, The Willows,** Barossa Valley, South Australia, £10.99, Australian Wine Club, OZ Wines
- 2001 **Carignane, Wild Hog Vineyard,** Dry Creek Valley, California, USA, £18, Villeneuve Wines

Mouthwatering, sweet-sour reds

Sounds weird? This style is the preserve of Italy, and
it's all about food: the rasp of sourness cuts through
rich, meaty food, with a lip-smacking tingle that works
equally well with pizza or tomato-based pasta dishes.
But there's fruit in there too – cherries and plums – plus raisiny
sweetness and a herby bite. The wines are now better made than
ever, with more seductive fruit, but holding on to those fascinating
flavours. You'll have to shell out up to a tenner for decent Chianti;
more for Piedmont wines (especially Barolo and Barbaresco, so try
Langhe instead). Valpolicella can be very good, but you need to
choose with care. Portugal can deliver something of the same
character with its sour-cherries reds. Oddball grapes like
Chambourcin often have these flavours.

- 2003 **Quinta das Setencostas,** Alenquer, Portugal, £5.99, Oddbins, Sainsbury's
- 1999 **Chianti Classico Riserva, Ampelos,** Tuscany, Italy, £6.98, Tesco
- 2001 **Shiraz-Sangiovese Il Briccone, Primo Estate,** Adelaide, South Australia, £9.99, Australian Wine Club, Harvey Nichols
- 2000 **Amarone della Valpolicella Classico, Vignale,** Veneto, Italy, £13.99, Waitrose
- 1999 **La Poja, Allegrini,** IGT Veronese, Italy, £37.99, Bennetts Fine Wines, Waitrose

Delicate (and not-so-delicate) rosé

Dry rosé can be wonderful, with flavours of strawberries and
maybe herbs. Look for wines from sturdy grapes like Cabernet,
Syrah or Merlot, or go for Grenache, the classic rosé grape of Spain
and the Rhône Valley. South America is a good, flavoursome bet.

- **2004 Syrah Rosé, Santa Julia,** Familia Zuccardi, Mendoza,
  Argentina, £4.99, Sainsbury's
- **2003 Côtes du Rhône Rosé, Enclave des Papes,** Rhône Valley,
  France, £4.99, Sainsbury's
- **2003 Bordeaux Rosé,
  Domaine de Sours,** Bordeaux, France, £5.49,
  Sainsbury's
- **2003 Costières de Nîmes
  Rosé, Domaine de St-
  Antoine,** France, £5.59,
  Oddbins
- **2003 Cabernet
  Sauvignon Rosé, Santa
  Rita,** Maipo, Chile, £5.85,
  Majestic, Oddbins,
  Sainsbury's

How to buy vegetarian and vegan wine

Virtually all wine is clarified with 'fining' agents, many of which
are animal by-products. Although they are not present in the
finished wine, they are clearly not acceptable for strict
vegetarians and vegans. Non-animal alternatives such as
bentonite clay are widely used and vegan wines rely solely on
these; vegetarian wines can use egg whites or milk proteins.
• **Specialist merchants** Organic specialists such as Vinceremos
and Vintage Roots assess every wine on their lists for its
vegetarian or vegan status.
• **Supermarkets** Most supermarkets stock some vegetarian and
vegan wines and identify own-label ones with a symbol, such as
the 'V' logo used by Somerfield and Marks & Spencer. Also look
for information on supermarket websites or contact the wine
department at the head office. They should be able to send a list
of all the vegetarian and vegan wines they sell.
• **Other outlets** Check the labels. Some producers, such as
Chapoutier, use a 'V' symbol to indicate vegetarian wines.

WHITE WINES
Bone-dry, neutral whites

Neutral wines exist for the sake of
seafood or to avoid interrupting you
while you're eating. It's a question of
balance, rather than aromas and
flavours, but there will be a bit of lemon,
yeast and a mineral thrill in a good
Muscadet sur lie or a proper Chablis. Loads
of Italian whites do the same thing, but Italy is
increasingly picking up on the global shift towards fruit flavours
and maybe some oak. Cheaper French wines are often too raw,
whereas low-priced Italian whites tend to be insipid. Basic, cheap
South African whites are often a good bet.

- 2004 Chardonnay Sur Lie, Danie de Wet, Robertson, South
  Africa, £4.04, Asda
- 2003 Viña Sol, Torres, Cataluña, Spain, £4.38, Asda
- 2002 Muscadet Sèvre et Maine sur lie, Château de la
  Mouchetière, Loire Valley, France, £4.99, Budgens
- 2003 Soave Classico, Vigneto Colombara, Zenato, Veneto,
  Italy, £4.99, Waitrose
- 2003 Chenin Blanc, Villiera, South Africa, £5.99, Co-op,
  Threshers, Unwins

Green, tangy whites

For nerve-tingling refreshment, Sauvignon Blanc is the classic
grape, full of fresh grass, gooseberry and nettle flavours. I always
used to go for New Zealand versions, but I'm now more inclined
to reach for an inexpensive bottle from South Africa or Hungary.
Or even a simple white Bordeaux, because suddenly Bordeaux
Sauvignon is buzzing with life. Most Sancerre and the other
Loire Sauvignons are overpriced. Austria's Grüner Veltliner has a
peppery freshness. Alternatively, look at Riesling. Australia
serves it up with bountiful lime and toast flavours while classic
German versions are steelier and green-apple fresh, with
intriguing peach and smoke flavours in their youth.

- 2003 Vin de Pays du Gers, Vignoble de Gascogne, South-
  West France, £3.49, Marks & Spencer
- 2003 Riesling, Tim Adams, Clare Valley, South Australia,
  £7.53, Tesco
- 2003 Sauvignon Blanc, Dashwood, Marlborough, New
  Zealand, £7.59, Oddbins
- 2002 Riesling, Gobelsburger, Kamptal, Austria, £7.75,
  Philglas & Swiggott, Wine Society
- 2003 Sauvignon Blanc, Fryer's Cove, Bamboes Bay, South
  Africa, £8.99, Anthony Byrne

Intense, nutty whites

The best white Burgundy from the Côte d'Or cannot be bettered for its combination of soft nut and oatmeal flavours, subtle, buttery oak and firm, dry structure. Prices are often hair-raising and the cheaper wines rarely offer much Burgundy style. For £6 or £7 your best bet is oaked Chardonnay from an innovative Spanish region such as Somontano or Navarra. You'll get a nutty, creamy taste and nectarine fruit with good oak-aged white Bordeaux or traditional white Rioja. Top Chardonnays from New World countries – and Italy for that matter – can emulate Burgundy, but once again we're looking at serious prices.

- 2002 Semillon, Mountain Vines, Cyprus, £4.29, Co-op
- 2002 Rioja, Torresoto, Compania Vinícola del Norte de Espana, Spain, £5.99, Marks & Spencer
- 2002 Chardonnay, Paul Cluver, Elgin, South Africa, £7.85, Christopher Piper, £9.95, La Réserve
- 2001 Bourgogne Chardonnay, Alex Gambal, Burgundy, France, £11.50, Mayfair Cellars
- 2001 Bourgogne Blanc, Domaine Galopierre, Burgundy, France, £14.99, Thresher

Ripe, toasty whites

Aussie Chardonnay conquered the world with its upfront flavours of peaches, apricots and tropical fruits, spiced up by the vanilla, toast and butterscotch richness of new oak. This winning style has now become a standard-issue flavour produced by all sorts of countries, though I still love the original. You don't need to spend more than a fiver for a great big friendly wine, though a well-spent £8 or so will give you more to relish beyond the second glass. Oaked Australian Semillon can also give rich, ripe fruit flavours. If you see the words 'unoaked' or 'cool-climate' on an Aussie bottle, expect an altogether leaner drink.

- 2001 Semillon, Peter Lehmann, Barossa Valley, South Australia, around £6, Flagship Wines, Oddbins, Unwins
- 2003 Marsanne-Viognier The Hermit Crab, d'Arenberg, McLaren Vale, South Australia, £7.49, Oddbins, £7.99 Booths
- 2002 Chardonnay Reserve, Denman Vineyard, Hunter Valley, New South Wales, Australia, £7.99, Tesco
- 2001 Chardonnay, Wither Hills, Marlborough, New Zealand, £8.99, Great Western Wine, Great Northern Wine, Oddbins, Wine Society
- 2002 Chardonnay, Montes Alpha, Casablanca Valley, Chile, £9.99, Hedley Wright, Majestic, Morrisons

Aromatic whites

Alsace has always been a plentiful source of perfumed, dry or off-dry whites: Gewürztraminer with its rose and lychee scent or Muscat with its floral, hothouse grape perfume. A few producers in New Zealand, Australia, Chile and South Africa are having some success with these grapes. Floral, apricotty Viognier, traditionally the grape of Condrieu in the northern Rhône, now appears in vins de pays from all over southern France and also from California and Australia. Condrieu is expensive (£20 will get you entry-level stuff and no guarantee that it will be fragrant); vin de pays wines start at around £5 and are just as patchy. Albariño from Rías Baixas in Spain is more reliable. For aroma on a budget grab some Hungarian Irsai Oliver or Argentinian Torrontes.

- 2003 **Matra Springs**, Hungary, £3.25, Waitrose
- 2002 **Viognier, Paul Mas**, Vin de Pays d'Oc, Languedoc-Roussillon, France, £5.52, Asda
- 2003 **Nótios, Gaia Estate**, Greece, £6.89, Oddbins
- 2003 **Gewürztraminer Visión, Cono Sur**, Chile, £7.99, Sainsbury's
- 2001 **Condrieu, Guigal**, Rhône Valley, France, £21–£26, Majestic, Tesco Wine Advisor Stores, Unwins

Golden, sweet whites

Good sweet wines are difficult to make and therefore expensive: prices for Sauternes and Barsac (from Bordeaux) can go through the roof, but near-neighbours Monbazillac, Loupiac, Saussignac and Ste-Croix-du-Mont are more affordable. Sweet Loire wines such as Quarts de Chaume, Bonnezeaux and some Vouvrays have a quince aroma and a fresh acidity that can keep them lively for decades, as do sweet Rieslings, such as Alsace Vendange Tardive, German and Austrian Beerenauslese (BA), Trockenbeerenauslese (TBA) and Eiswein. Canadian icewine is quite rare over here, but we're seeing more of Hungary's Tokaji, with its sweet-sour, marmalade flavours.

- 2002 **Coteaux du Layon-Chaume, Domaine des Forges**, Loire Valley, France, £8.99/50 cl, Waitrose
- 2001 **Botrytis Riesling-Gewürztraminer, La Magia, Joseph Primo Estate**, South Australia, £12/half bottle, Harvey Nichols
- 2001 **Sauternes, Château Liot**, Bordeaux, France, £9.79/half bottle, Waitrose
- 1999 **De Bortoli Noble One Botrytis Semillon**, New South Wales, Australia, £12.99/half bottle, O W Loeb, Noble Rot
- 2001 **Scheurebe TBA No. 9, Kracher**, Austria, £30.99/half bottle, Noel Young Wines

SPARKLING WINES

Champagne can be the finest sparkling wine on the planet, but fizz made by the traditional Champagne method in Australia, New Zealand or California – often using the same grape varieties – is often just as good and cheaper. It might be a little more fruity, where Champagne concentrates on bready, yeasty or nutty aromas, but a few are dead ringers for the classic style. Fizz is also made in other parts of France: Crémant de Bourgogne is one of the best. England is beginning to show its potential. Spain's Cava is perfect party fizz available at bargain basement prices in all the big supermarkets.

- **NV Pelorus,** Cloudy Bay, Marlborough, New Zealand, £13.75 Majestic, £13.99 Unwins
- **1996 Blanc de Blancs, Nyetimber,** West Sussex, England, £20, Ballantynes of Cowbridge, Berry Bros. & Rudd
- **NV Jansz,** Australia, £9.99 Noble Rot, £10.99 Oddbins, Philglas & Swiggot, Selfridges
- **Champagne Brut Réserve, Mis en Cave en 1998, Charles Heidsieck,** France, £23.49, Waitrose
- **1996 Champagne Lanson Gold Label,** about £28, Morrisons, Sainsbury's, Tesco, Thresher, Waitrose

FORTIFIED WINES
Tangy, appetizing fortified wines

To set your taste buds tingling, fino and manzanilla sherries are pale, perfumed, bone-dry and bracingly tangy. True amontillado, dark and nutty, is also dry. Dry oloroso adds deep, raisiny flavours. Palo cortado falls somewhere between amontillado and oloroso, and manzanilla pasada is an older, nuttier style of manzanilla.

The driest style of Madeira, Sercial, is steely and smoky; Verdelho Madeira is a bit fuller and richer, but still tangy and dry.

- **Manzanilla La Gitana,** Hidalgo, about £6, widely available
- **Manzanilla Mariscal,** Dolores Bustillo Delgado, £6.65, Tanners
- **Amontillado Del Duque,** González Byass, £11–12/half bottle, Sainsbury's, Villeneuve Wines
- **Amontillado Principe de Barbadillo,** £19.99, Connolly's, Stevens Garnier
- **10 Year Old Sercial Madeira,** Henriques & Henriques, £16.99/50 cl, Majestic, Waitrose, Tanners, Noel Young Wines

Rich, warming fortified wines

Raisins and brown sugar, dried figs and caramelized nuts – do you like the sound of that? Port is the classic dark sweet wine, and it comes in several styles, from basic ruby, to tawny, matured in cask for 10 years or more, to vintage, which matures to mellowness in the bottle. The Portuguese island of Madeira produces fortified wines with rich brown smoky flavours and a startling bite of acidity: the sweet styles to look for are Bual and Malmsey.

Decent sweet sherries are rare; oloroso dulce is a style with stunningly concentrated flavours. In southern France, Banyuls and Maury are deeply fruity fortified wines. Marsala, from Sicily, has rich brown sugar flavours with a refreshing sliver of acidity. The versatile Muscat grape makes luscious golden wines all around the Mediterranean, but also pops up in orange, black, and the gloriously rich, treacly brown versions that Australia does superbly.

- **1997 Samos Anthemis**, Greece, £7.99 Eclectic Wines (www.eclecticwines.com, 020 7736 3733), £8.75, Wine Society
- **Noé Very Old Pedro Ximénez**, González Byass, £11–12/half bottle, Tesco, Villeneuve Wines
- **Rich Oloroso Sherry, East India Solera**, Lustau, Spain, £10.99, Sainsbury's, Waitrose
- **Quinta do Noval, 10-year-old Tawny Port**, Portugal, £15.25 Waitrose
- **15 Year Old Malmsey Madeira**, Henriques & Henriques, £16.49/50 cl, Tanners, Waitrose, Noel Young Wines
- **Rutherglen Grand Muscat**, Chambers Rosewood Vineyards, Victoria, Australia, £21.95/half bottle, Lay & Wheeler

Wine to go

We're lucky in the UK to have a huge choice of wines right on our doorstep – or just a phone call or mouse-click away. But if you're anything like me, sometimes the spirit of adventure will take hold, and you'll just have to stride out and explore the world of wine for yourself.

DAY TRIPPER
Cross-Channel wine shopping is hugely popular with us Brits – and no wonder, when UK duty is £1.23 on a bottle of still wine, while in France it's 2p (the difference is even greater on sparkling wines) – there are fantastic savings to be made.

Calais accounts for around 80% of all our booze-buying in France: it has the widest choice of sea crossings, four hypermarkets, 12 supermarkets and numerous wine warehouses, some of them in the huge Cité d'Europe shopping complex next to the Eurotunnel terminal.

There are no limits on the amount of wine you can bring back, as long as it is for personal consumption – you can fill a van for a party, but you may be questioned at customs if you try to bring back more than 90 litres (10 cases of 12 bottles). Wine bottles are heavy, so don't overload your car.

HEADING SOUTH
Many of us visit France, Spain and Italy on holiday, and I can think of few greater pleasures for wine lovers than tasting wine in the place it's made. It's a wonderful way to learn about wine and who knows, you might come across something that *we* haven't discovered.

WHERE TO GO
Alsace, Burgundy and the Loire are perhaps the most delightful regions for the wine lover, but wherever vines are grown in France you're likely to see signs

---

CALAIS
If you're mainly looking to save money, the UK store outlets have the advantage of familiarity. Use their websites to check out what's available before you go. You can also pre-order online and collect on the day, giving you more time for lunch or stocking up on French cheeses. Some are closed on Sunday.

- ✪ Majestic has 3 French outlets called Wine & Beer World (see page 141) www.wineandbeer.co.uk
- ✪ www.oddbins.com
- ✪ www.sainsburys.co.uk/calais
- ✪ www.tesco.com/vinplus
- ✪ www.day-tripper.net has masses of information on cross-Channel shopping for visitors to Calais.

A little bit Of France for a lot less than you think!

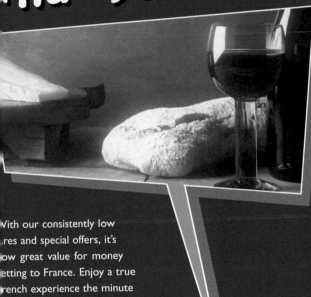

With our consistently low ~~fa~~res and special offers, it's ~~n~~ow great value for money ~~g~~etting to France. Enjoy a true ~~F~~rench experience the minute ~~y~~ou get onboard with our ~~s~~tylish décor and selection ~~o~~f individual restaurants, ~~c~~afes and bars. So for that ~~j~~e ne sais quoi, think SeaFrance.

A little bit of France no one else can offer!

SEAFRANCE
DOVER·CALAIS FERRIES

by the roadside saying *'dégustation et vente'* (tasting and sales) or *'vente directe'* (direct sales). Follow the sign and you might end up at a château or an industrial-looking co-operative. In Bordeaux, by all means visit the famous châteaux, but it's the less famous ones that will welcome you in, and even then you'll be shocked at the prices. In Champagne, most of the big houses in Reims and Epernay do guided tours.

Cantinas (wine cellars) can be found all over Italy, but Piedmont, Tuscany and the Veneto are the regions that have been at it longest, and are most geared up for tourists. The local *consorzio* (group of growers) might organize wine tours – check at the town tourist office. If you're on the road, look for signs saying *vendita diretta* (direct sales) or *degustazione* (tasting). Also look out for an *enoteca* (wine bar/shop): the one in the stadium on the edge of Siena boasts scores of Chianti.

In Spain you'll find bodegas set up to welcome tourists in three main regions: Rioja, about 90 km (60 miles) south-east of Bilbao; Penedès, 30 km (20 miles) inland from Barcelona, the most important region for the production of cava fizz; and down in Andalucía you'll find it hard to avoid visiting at least one sherry bodega in the town of Jerez.

TASTING TIPS

Don't expect to find an English speaker, but a few words of the local language go a long way. In France it's good manners when entering a room to greet people with *'Bonjour, Monsieur/ Madame'*. Don't feel you have to buy, even if you taste – just say *merci beaucoup* before you leave.

In Italy a liberal use of *buon giorno* (good day), *bella* (beautiful) and *grazie* (thank you) will win friends.

In Spain, smooth your path with *buenos días* (good morning), *buenas tardes* (good afternoon), *gracias* (thank you); *vino tinto* means red wine.

Remember that lunchtimes are important in Europe: the French often close for 2 hours, and the Italians and Spanish for even longer.

WEBSITES FOR WINE TOURISM

- ✪ www.check-in-france.com – the 'tradition & art of living' section has touring routes through all French wine regions.
- ✪ www.wosa.co.za – includes maps and touring routes for all South Africa's wine regions.
- ✪ www.australia.com – features an overview of Australian wine and links to detailed regional websites.
- ✪ www.newzealand.com – 'Michael Cooper's Wine Tour' includes introductions, history, touring information and festival dates for all NZ wine regions.
- ✪ www.travelenvoy.com/wine/siteindex.htm – details for just about every winery in the USA.
- ✪ www.english-wine-producers.co.uk – contains useful maps and details for visitors.

SPECIALIST WINE TOURS

Specialist wine tours are a fantastic way to learn about wine in a way you'll never forget, and it's all done for you – visits planned, experts to show you around, translators on hand. Established companies such as Arblaster & Clarke have the experience to help you get the most out of your visit.

THE LONG HAUL

Wine tourists in South Africa, Australia, New Zealand and California are well catered for, by friendly people who speak our language.

Cape Town is a great base from which to explore South Africa's most important vineyard regions: Stellenbosch, Paarl and Constantia.

In Australia the big cities of Adelaide, Sydney and Melbourne all have top wine destinations within easy reach. Most famous of all is the Hunter Valley near Sydney. Melbourne has the Yarra Valley and Mornington Peninsula within an hour or so's drive. Adelaide is the best wine city, with Barossa Valley and McLaren Vale to the north and south and Adelaide Hills to the east.

In New Zealand's important regions, such as Hawkes Bay, Martinborough and Marlborough, the wineries are fairly close together. Look for a magazine called *Cuisine Wine Country*, with all the details you need to visit over 400 wineries, plus places to eat and stay.

California's Napa Valley is well set up for tourists, but is not cheap. Just over the mountains to the west is Sonoma County, which is less commercialized, more friendly, and has a wider range of wines. If you're feeling adventurous, head for Amador County, the old gold-mining region nestling in the Sierra Nevada mountains.

CLOSE TO HOME

There are some 350 vineyards in England and Wales. English wine is getting better and better, and the very hot 2003 vintage produced some super whites and reds. Sparkling wines are beginning to challenge Champagne for quality; find your local vineyard and see for yourself.

Buying for the long term

Most of this book is about wines to drink more or less immediately – that's how modern wines are made, and that's what you'll find in most high street retail outlets. If you're looking for a mature vintage of a great wine that's ready to drink – or are prepared to wait 10 years or more for a great vintage to reach its peak – specialist wine merchants will be able to help; the internet's another good place to look for mature wines. Here's my beginners' guide to buying wine at auction and *en primeur*.

AUCTIONS

A catalogue from either of the UK's top wine auction houses, Christie's and Sotheby's, will have wine enthusiasts drooling over the prestigious names that are virtually unobtainable elsewhere. Better still, the lots are often of mature vintages that are ready to drink. Before you go, find out all you can about the producer and vintages described in the catalogue. My *Pocket Wine Book* is a good place to start, or Michael Broadbent's *Vintage Wines* for old and rare wines, and the national wine magazines (*Decanter, Wine International*) run regular features on wine regions and their vintages. This is important – some merchants take the opportunity to clear inferior vintages at auction.

The drawbacks? You have no guarantee that the wine has been well stored, and if it's faulty you have little chance of redress. But for expensive and mature wines, I have to say that the top auction houses nowadays make a considerable effort to check the provenance and integrity of the wines. As prices of the most sought-after wines have soared, so it has become profitable either to forge the bottles and their contents or to try to pass off stock that is clearly out of condition. And don't forget that there will be a commission to pay. Online wine auctions have similar pros and cons.

BUYING EN PRIMEUR

En primeur is a French term for wine which is sold before it is bottled, sometimes referred to as a 'future'. In the spring after the vintage the Bordeaux châteaux – and a few other wine-producing regions – hold tastings of barrel samples for members of the international wine trade. The châteaux then offer a proportion of their production to the wine merchants (*négociants*) in Bordeaux, who in turn offer it to wine merchants around the world at an opening price. The advantage to the châteaux is that their capital is not tied up in expensive stock for the next year or two, until the wines are bottled and ready to ship.

Traditionally merchants would buy *en primeur* for stock to be sold later at a higher price, while offering their customers the chance to take advantage of the opening prices as well. The idea of private individuals investing rather than institutions took off with a series of good Bordeaux vintages in the 1980s.

WINE FOR THE FUTURE

There is a lot to be said for buying *en primeur*. For one thing, in a great vintage you may be able to find the finest and rarest wines far more cheaply than they will ever appear again. This was especially true of the 1990 vintage in Bordeaux; this, in turn, primed the market for the exceptional vintages of 1999 in Burgundy and 2000 in Bordeaux. Equally, when a wine – even a relatively inexpensive one – is made in very limited quantities, buying *en primeur* may be practically your only chance of getting hold of it.

In the past, British wine merchants and their privileged customers were able to 'buy double what you want, sell half for double what you paid, and drink for free', but as the market has opened up to people more interested in making a quick buck than drinking fine wine, the whole process has become more risky.

Prices can go down as well as up. They may easily not increase significantly in the few years after the campaign.

Some popular vintages are offered at ridiculously high prices – some unpopular ones too. It's only about twice a decade that the combination of high quality and fair prices offers the private buyer a chance of a good, guaranteed profit. Interestingly, if one highly touted vintage is followed by another, the prices for the second one often have to fall because the market simply will not accept two inflated price structures in a row. Recent Bordeaux examples of this are the excellent 1990 after the much hyped 1989 and the potentially fine 2001 after the understandably hyped 2000.

During the past year there has been a lot of ballyhoo about Burgundy's 2002 vintage and Bordeaux's 2003. Across the board there are lovely Burgundies in 2002 – but buy them to drink: they will rarely appreciate in price. 2003 Bordeaux is a result of the hotter ripening conditions. Interestingly, the heavier, less classic clay soils of the Médoc made many of the best wines, and at reasonable prices. Well-known Médoc wines as well as St-Émilions and Pomerols are very patchy in quality and frequently absurd in price. It is already far too late to invest in 2003 for profit, but less popular wines won't rise in value and will be available for a while yet.

Another potential hazard is that a tasting assessment is difficult at an early date. There is a well-founded suspicion that many barrel samples are doctored (legally) to appeal to the most powerful consumer critics, in particular the American Robert Parker and *The Wine Spectator* magazine. The wine that is finally bottled may or may not bear a resemblance to what was tasted in the spring following the vintage. In any case, most serious red wines are in a difficult stage of their evolution in the spring, and with the best will in the world it is possible to get one's evaluation wrong. However, the aforementioned Americans, and magazines like *Wine International* and *Decanter* will do their best to offer you accurate judgements on the newly offered wines, and most merchants who make a *primeur* offer also write a good assessment of the wines. You will find that many of them quote the Parker or *Wine Spectator* marks. Anything over 90 out of 100 risks being hyped and hiked in price. Many of the best bargains get marks between 85 and 89, since the 90+ marks are generally awarded for power rather than subtlety. Consideration can be given to the producer's reputation for consistency and to the general vintage assessment for the region.

SECURE CELLARAGE

Another worry is that the merchant you buy the wine from may not still be around to deliver it to you two years later. Buy from a merchant you trust, with a solid trading base in other wines.

Once the wines are shipped you may want your merchant to store the wine for you. If so, you should insist that (1) you receive a stock certificate; (2) your wines are stored separately from the merchant's own stocks; and (3) your cases are identifiable as your property and are labelled accordingly. All good merchants offer these safeguards as a minimum service.

CHECK THE SMALL PRINT

Traditional wine merchants may quote prices exclusive of VAT and/or duty: wine may not be the bargain it first appears.

A wine quoted *en primeur* is usually offered on an ex-cellars (EC) basis; the price excludes shipping, duties and taxes such as VAT. A price quoted in bond (IB) in the UK includes shipping, but excludes duties and taxes.

SPECIALIST MERCHANTS OFFERING 'EN PRIMEUR'

Full details for these merchants can be found in our retailers directory, starting on page 106

- ✪ Adnams, John Armit, Averys
- ✪ Ballantynes, Bancroft, Bennetts, Berry Bros & Rudd, Bibendum, Bordeaux Index, Butlers, Anthony Byrne, D Byrne
- ✪ Cave Cru Classé, ChâteauOnline, Cockburns of Leith, Connolly's, Corney & Barrow
- ✪ Direct Wine Shipments, Domaine Direct
- ✪ Farr Vintners, Fortnum & Mason, Friarwood
- ✪ Gauntleys, Goedhuis, Great Western Wine
- ✪ Jeroboams, S H Jones, Justerini & Brooks
- ✪ Lay & Wheeler, Lea & Sandeman, O W Loeb
- ✪ Martinez Wines, Mayfair Cellars, Millésima, Montrachet, Morris & Verdin
- ✪ James Nicholson, Nickolls & Perks
- ✪ Christopher Piper, Playford Ros, Portland Wine
- ✪ Raeburn Fine Wine, La Réserve, Howard Ripley, Roberson
- ✪ Savage Selection, Tanners
- ✪ Wimbledon Wine Cellar, The Wine Society, Peter Wylie, Noel Young Wines

Retailers directory

All these retailers have been chosen on the basis of the quality and interest of their lists. If you want to find local suppliers, retailers are listed by region in the Who's Where directory on page 144.

> The following services are available where indicated:
> **C** = cellarage **G** = glass hire/loan
> **M** = mail order **T** = tastings and talks

A & B Vintners

Little Tawsden, Spout Lane, Brenchley, Kent TN12 7AS (01892) 724977 FAX (01892) 722673 E-MAIL info@abvintners.co.uk WEBSITE www.abvintners.co.uk HOURS Mon–Fri 9–6 CARDS MasterCard, Visa DELIVERY Free 5 cases or more, otherwise £11.75 per consignment UK mainland MINIMUM ORDER 1 mixed case EN PRIMEUR Bandol, Burgundy, Languedoc, Rhône. **C M T**
✪ Star attractions *Impressive list with a string of top-quality domaines from Burgundy and the Rhône, and little-known gems from the Languedoc and Bandol.*

Adnams

HEAD OFFICE & MAIL ORDER
Sole Bay Brewery, Southwold, Suffolk IP18 6JW (01502) 727222 FAX (01502) 727223 E-MAIL wines@adnams.co.uk WEBSITE www.adnamswines.co.uk SHOPS The Wine Cellar & Kitchen Store, Victoria Street, Southwold, Suffolk IP18 6JW • The Wine Shop, Pinkney's Lane, Southwold, Suffolk IP18 6EW HOURS (Orderline) Mon–Fri 9–8, Sat 9–5; Wine Cellar & Kitchen Store and Wine Shop: Mon–Sat 9–6, Sun 11–4 CARDS MasterCard, Switch, Visa DISCOUNTS 5% for 5 cases or more DELIVERY

Free for complete cases, £7.50 part cases in most of mainland UK MINIMUM ORDER (Mail order) 1 case EN PRIMEUR Bordeaux, Burgundy, Port, Rhône, Sauternes. **G M T**
✪ Star attractions *Top names from most regions of France, such as Étienne Sauzet in Burgundy and René Rostaing in the Rhône. Characterful producers from the New World include Ridge (California), Yarra Yering and Mitchell (Australia), Forrest Estate and Martinborough Vineyards (New Zealand). Telmo Rodríguez, one of Spain's top winemakers, is well represented.*

Aldi Stores

PO Box 26, Atherstone, Warwickshire CV9 2SH; 270 stores STORE LOCATION LINE 08705 134262 WEBSITE www.aldi-stores.co.uk HOURS Mon–Wed 9–6, Thurs–Fri 9–7, Sat 8.30–5.30, Sun 10–4 (selected stores) CARDS Switch, Visa (debit only)
✪ Star attractions *Aldi have some terrific bargains from around the world, with lots available under £3, but can also push the boat out for decent claret.*

Amey's Wines

83 Melford Road, Sudbury, Suffolk CO10 1JT (01787) 377144

HOURS Tue–Fri 9–5; Sat 9–4 **CARDS** AmEx, MasterCard, Switch, Visa **DISCOUNTS** 10% for a mixed dozen, 15% for 5 or more mixed cases **DELIVERY** Free within 10 miles of Sudbury for orders over £60. **G T**
✪ Star attractions *Expect the unexpected in this well-chosen list of characterful wines: Gérard Depardieu's Condrieu (£19.99) rubs shoulders with Barbadillo's sherries, Montes Alpha Syrah from Chile (£11.99) and Penfolds Grange from Australia (£109).*

John Armit Wines

5 Royalty Studios, 105 Lancaster Road, London W11 1QF (020) 7908 0600 **FAX** (020) 7908 0601 **E-MAIL** info@armit.co.uk **WEBSITE** www.armit.co.uk **HOURS** Mon–Fri 9–6 **CARDS** MasterCard, Switch, Visa **DELIVERY** Free for orders over £180, otherwise £15 delivery charge **MINIMUM ORDER** 1 case **EN PRIMEUR** Bordeaux, Burgundy, Italy, Rhône. **C M T**
✪ Star attractions *Classy merchant with a star-studded list that's particularly strong in Italy, Burgundy and the Rhône, with some gems from Germany, Spain and the New World. For everyday drinking the own-label range comes from some great winemakers, including clarets from Mouiex and South African red and white from Steenberg.*

ASDA

HEAD OFFICE Asda House, Southbank, Great Wilson Street, Leeds LS11 5AD (0113) 243 5435 **FAX** (0113) 241 8666 **CUSTOMER SERVICE** (0500) 100055; 266 stores **WEBSITE** www.asda.co.uk **HOURS** Selected stores open 24 hrs, see local store for details **CARDS** MasterCard, Switch, Visa **DISCOUNTS** Buy 6 bottles, save 5%, case deals: 10% off price including delivery **DELIVERY** Selected stores. **T**

✪ Star attractions *Good-value basics – with lots under a fiver – but in the past year they've expanded their range and there is a welcome increase in the number of interesting wines at £7+.*

L'Assemblage

Pallant Court, 10 West Pallant, Chichester, West Sussex PO19 1TG (01243) 537775 **FAX** (01243) 538644 **E-MAIL** sales@lassemblage.co.uk **WEBSITE** www.lassemblage.co.uk **HOURS** Mon–Fri 9.30–6 **CARDS** MasterCard, Switch, Visa **DELIVERY** Free for overs over £500 **MINIMUM ORDER** 1 case **EN PRIMEUR** Bordeaux, Burgundy, Port, Italy. **C M T**
✪ Star attractions *A fascinating list of fine wines, mostly from classic regions of France, especially Burgundy. Blue-chip wines at blue-chip prices.*

Australian Wine Club

MAIL ORDER PO Box 3079, Datchet, Slough SL3 9LZ 0800 856 2004 FAX 0800 856 2114 E-MAIL orders@australianwine.co.uk WEBSITE www.australianwine.co.uk HOURS Mon–Fri 8am–9pm, Sat–Sun 9–6 CARDS AmEx, MasterCard, Switch, Visa, Diners DELIVERY £4.99 anywhere in UK mainland MINIMUM ORDER 1 mixed case EN PRIMEUR Australia. M T
✪ Star attractions *The original mail-order Aussie wine specialist, buzzing with top names.*

Averys Wine Merchants

4 High Street, Nailsea, Bristol BS48 1BT TEL (01275) 811100 FAX (01275) 811101 ORDERLINE 08451 283797 E-MAIL sales@averys.com • Shop and Cellar, 9 Culver Street, Bristol, BS1 5LD (0117) 921 4146/5 E-MAIL cellars@averys.com HOURS Mon–Sat 10–7 CARDS AmEx, MasterCard, Switch, Visa DISCOUNTS Monthly mail order offers, Discover Wine with Averys 13th bottle free DELIVERY £4.95 per delivery address EN PRIMEUR Bordeaux, Burgundy, Port. C G M T
✪ Star attractions *A small but very respectable selection from just about everywhere in France, Italy and Germany. Spain looks promising and there's some good New World stuff, such as Felton Road from New Zealand.*

Bacchus Wine

Warrington House Farm Barn, Warrington, Olney, Bucks MK46 4HN (01234) 711140 FAX (01234) 711199 E-MAIL wine@bacchus.co.uk WEBSITE www.bacchus.co.uk HOURS Mon–Fri 10.30–6.30, Sat 10.30–2 CARDS AmEx, Diners, MasterCard, Switch, Visa DELIVERY Free within 10 miles of Olney; elsewhere £10 1 case; £5 subsequent cases (maximum charge £20) MINIMUM ORDER 1 mixed case. G M T

✪ Star attractions *One of the largest lists of Austrian wines, both red and white, in the UK. Splendid stuff from Italy, Burgundy – in fact from most of France – Spain, North and South America and South Africa There are plenty of unusual choices A 'revolutionary pricing policy' puts most wines between £6 and £20.*

Ballantynes of Cowbridge

3 Westgate, Cowbridge, Vale of Glamorgan CF71 7AQ (01446) 774840 FAX (01446) 775253 E-MAIL richard@ballantynes.co.uk WEBSITE www.ballantynes.co.uk • 211–17 Cathedral Road, Cardiff, CF11 9PP (02920) 222202 HOURS Mon–Sat 9–5.30 CARDS MasterCard, Switch, Visa DISCOUNTS 8% per case DELIVERY £9.99 for first case; £4.99 for subsequent cases EN PRIMEUR Bordeaux, Burgundy, Italy, Rhône. C G M T
✪ Star attractions *Italy, Burgundy and Languedoc-Roussillon are stunning, most regions of France are well represented, and there's some terrific stuff from Australia, New Zealand, Spain, California – even Oregon gets a look-in.*

Balls Brothers

313 Cambridge Heath Road, London E2 9LQ (020) 7739 6466 FAX 0870 243 9775 DIRECT SALES (020) 7739 1642 E-MAIL wine@ballsbrothers.co.uk WEBSITE www.ballsbrothers.co.uk HOURS Mon–Fri 9–5.30 CARDS AmEx, Diners, MasterCard, Switch, Visa DELIVERY Free 1 case or more locally; £8 1 case, free 2 cases or more, England, Wales and Scottish Lowlands; islands and Scottish Highlands phone for details. G M T
✪ Star attractions *French specialist – you'll find something of interest from most regions – with older vintages available. Spain and Australia are also very good. Many of the wines can be enjoyed in Balls Brothers' London wine bars.*

H & H Bancroft Wines

1 China Wharf, 29 Mill Street, London SE1 2BQ (020) 7232 5450 **FAX** (020) 7232 5451 **E-MAIL** sales@handhbancroftwines.com **WEBSITE** www.handhbancroft wines.com **HOURS** Mon–Fri 9–5.30 **CARDS** Delta, MasterCard, Switch, Visa **DISCOUNTS** Negotiable **DELIVERY** £11.75 for 1–2 cases in mainland UK; free 3 cases or more **MINIMUM ORDER** 1 case **EN PRIMEUR** Bordeaux, Burgundy, Rhône. **C M T**
✪ **Star attractions** *Bancroft are UK agents for an impressive flotilla of French winemakers: Burgundy, Rhône, Loire and some interesting wines from southern France. Italy looks promising, too. A separate fine wine list includes Bordeaux back to 1945, plus top names from Burgundy and the Rhône.*

Bat & Bottle

MAIL ORDER 9 Ashwell Road, Oakham, Rutland LE15 6QG 0845 108 4407 **FAX** 0870 458 2505 **E-MAIL** post@batwine.co.uk **WEBSITE** www.batwine.co.uk **HOURS** Mon–Fri 8.30–5.30, out-of-hours answering maching **CARDS** MasterCard, Switch, Visa **MINIMUM ORDER** 1 mixed case. **G M T**
✪ **Star attractions** *Ben and Emma Robson specialize in Italy, and in characterful wines from small producers discovered on their regular visits to the country. An inspired and inspiring list.*

Bennetts Fine Wines

High Street, Chipping Campden, Glos GL55 6AG (01386) 840392 **FAX** (01386) 840974 **E-MAIL** enquiries@bennettsfinewines.com **WEBSITE** www.bennettsfinewines.com **HOURS** Mon–Fri 10–6, Sat 9–6 **CARDS** MasterCard, Switch, Visa **DISCOUNTS** On collected orders of 1 case or more **DELIVERY** £6 per case, minimum charge £12 **EN PRIMEUR** Burgundy, California, Rhône, Italy, New Zealand. **G M T**

✪ **Star attractions** *I couldn't find much under £5 here, but I wouldn't really expect to, given the calibre of the producers. France and Italy have the lion's share, but Germany, Spain and Portugal look good too. New World wines are similarly high up the quality scale, with the likes of Kumeu River and Isabel Estate from New Zealand, Plantagenet and Cullen from Australia, Seghesio from California and Domaine Drouhin from Oregon.*

Berkmann Wine Cellars

10–12 Brewery Road, London N7 9NH (020) 7609 4711 **FAX** (020) 7607 0018 • Brian Coad Wine Cellars, 41b Valley Road, Plympton, Plymouth, Devon PL7 1RF (01752) 334970 • Pagendam Pratt Wine Cellars, 16 Marston Moor Business Park, Rudgate, Tockwith, N. Yorks YO26 7QF (01423) 337567
• T M Robertson Wine Cellars, 10 Lower Gilmore Place, Edinburgh EH3 9PA (0131) 229 4522 **E-MAIL** info@berkmann.co.uk **WEBSITE** www.berkmann.co.uk **HOURS** Mon–Fri 9–5.30 **CARDS** MasterCard, Switch, Visa **DISCOUNTS** £3 per unmixed case collected **DELIVERY** Free for orders over £100 to UK mainland (excluding the Highlands) **MINIMUM ORDER** 1 mixed case. **C G M**
✪ **Star attractions** *Berkmann is the UK agent for, among others, Antinori, Maculan, Mastroberardino, Masi and Tasca d'Almerita, so there are some fab Italian wines here. New World wines include some top stuff from Australia, New Zealand and South Africa, plus Stags' Leap from California and Chateau Ste Michelle from Washington. But France hasn't been forgotten: affordable claret and Burgundy, Alsace from René Muré and Beaujolais from Duboeuf. Loire wines include Sancerre from Crochet and Pouilly-Fumé from Dagueneau.*

Berry Bros. & Rudd

3 St James's Street, London SW1A 1EG (020) 7396 9600 **FAX** (020) 7396 9611 **ORDERS OFFICE** 0870 900 4300 (lines open Mon–Fri 9–6, Sat 10–4) **ORDERS FAX** 0870 900 4301
• Berrys' Wine Shop, Hamilton Close, Houndmills, Basingstoke, Hants RG21 6YB (01256) 323566
• Terminal 3 departures, Heathrow Airport, TW6 1JH (020) 8564 8361
• Terminal 4 departures, Heathrow, TW6 3XA (020) 8754 1961 **E-MAIL** orders@bbr.com **WEBSITE** www.bbr.com **HOURS** St James's Street: Mon–Fri 9–6, Sat 10–4; Berrys' Wine Shop: Mon–Thur 10–6, Fri 10–8, Sat 10–4; Heathrow: Daily 6am–10pm **CARDS** AmEx, Diners, MasterCard, Switch, Visa **DISCOUNTS** Variable **DELIVERY** Free for orders of £150 or more, otherwise £10 **EN PRIMEUR** Bordeaux, Burgundy, Rhône. **C G M T**
✪ **Star attractions** *The shop in St James's is the very image of a traditional wine merchant, but Berry Bros. also has one of the best websites around. The Blue List covers old, rare fine wines while the main list is both classy and wide-ranging: there's an emphasis on the classic regions of France; smaller but equally tempting selections from just about everywhere else. Not everything is expensive: Berrys' Own Selection is extensive and includes, for example, a French Country White (£4.75) made for them by Yves Grassa.*

Bibendum Wine

113 Regents Park Road, London NW1 8UR (020) 7449 4120 **FAX** (020) 7449 4121 **E-MAIL** sales@bibendum-wine.co.uk **WEBSITE** www.bibendum-wine.co.uk **HOURS** Mon–Fri 9–6 **CARDS** MasterCard, Switch, Visa **DELIVERY** Free throughout mainland UK for orders over £250, otherwise £15 **EN PRIMEUR** Bordeaux, Burgundy, New World, Rhône, Port. **G M T**
✪ **Star attractions** *Bibendum looks for wines that nobody else is shipping – although that's not to say you won't find them elsewhere, since Bibendum supply the trade as well as private customers. Equally strong in the Old World and the New: Huet in Vouvray, Lageder in Alto Adige and Brundlmayer in Austria are matched by d'Arenberg, Chain of Ponds and Katnook from Australia, and a full range from Catena Zapata of Argentina.*

Booths Supermarkets

4 Fishergate, Preston PR1 3LJ (01772) 251701 **FAX** (01772) 204316; 27 stores across the North of England **E-MAIL** admin@booths-supermarkets.co.uk **WEBSITE** www.booths-supermarkets.co.uk, and www.booths-wine.co.uk **HOURS** Office: Mon–Fri 8.30–5; shop hours vary **CARDS** AmEx, Electron, MasterCard, Switch, Solo, Visa **DISCOUNTS** 5% off any 6 bottles. **G T**
✪ **Star attractions** *A list for any merchant to be proud of, never mind a supermarket. There's plenty under £4, but if you're occasionally prepared to hand over £7–9 you'll find some really interesting stuff.*

Bordeaux Index

MAIL ORDER 6th Floor, 159–173 St John Street, London EC1V 4QJ (020) 7253 2110 **FAX** (020) 7490 1995 **E-MAIL** sales@bordeauxindex.com **WEBSITE** www.bordeauxindex.com **HOURS** Mon–Fri 8.30–6 **CARDS** AmEx, MasterCard, Switch, Visa, JCB (transaction fees apply) **DELIVERY** (Private sales only) free for orders over £2,000 UK mainland; others at cost **MINIMUM ORDER** £500 **EN PRIMEUR** Bordeaux, Burgundy, Rhône, Italy. **C M T**
✪ **Star attractions** *A serious list for serious spenders. Pages and pages of red Bordeaux, dating back to 1900, and, in spite of the company name, stacks of top Burgundies and Rhônes. Spain, Portugal, Italy and*

Australia have smaller selections, with the focus on classic names. And there's Cloudy Bay from New Zealand.

Budgens Stores

HEAD OFFICE Stonefield Way, Ruislip, Middlesex HA4 0JR (020) 8422 9511 FAX (020) 8864 2800, for nearest store call 0800 526002; 234 stores mainly in Southern England and East Anglia E-MAIL info@ budgens.co.uk WEBSITE www.budgens.co.uk HOURS Vary according to location (55 stores open 24 hours); usually Mon–Sat 8–8, Sun 10–4 CARDS MasterCard, Solo, Switch, Visa. **G**
✪ **Star attractions** *You can feel reasonably confident of going into a store and coming out with some wine you'd actually like to drink these days, at bargain-basement prices upwards.*

The Butlers Wine Cellar

247 Queens Park Road, Brighton BN2 9XJ (01273) 698724 FAX (01273) 622761 E-MAIL henry@butlers-winecellar.co.uk WEBSITE www.butlers-winecellar.co.uk HOURS Tue–Wed 10–6, Thur–Sat 10–7 CARDS AmEx, MasterCard, Switch, Visa DELIVERY Free locally 1 case or more; free UK mainland 3 cases or more EN PRIMEUR Bordeaux. **G M T**
✪ **Star attractions** *To get full value from this list you'll need to look at the website or join the mailing list: it's the odds and ends that are the main point, and they change all the time, but include French, Italian and Spanish vintages back to the 1960s. The main list is short but irresistible, with the likes of Anselmi from Italy, Breaky Bottom from England, Quinta de la Rosa port and a sherry for all tastes. Lucky Brighton.*

Anthony Byrne

MAIL ORDER Ramsey Business Park, Stocking Fen Road, Ramsey, Cambs PE26 2UR (01487) 814555 FAX (01487) 814962 E-MAIL anthony@ abfw.co.uk or claude@abfw.co.uk WEBSITE www.abfw.co.uk HOURS Mon–Fri 9–5.30 CARDS None DISCOUNTS available on cases DELIVERY Free 5 cases or more, or orders of £250 or more; otherwise £6 MINIMUM ORDER 1 case EN PRIMEUR Bordeaux, Burgundy, Champagne, Rhône. **C M T**
✪ **Star attractions** *A serious list of Burgundy; Loire from top growers such as Serge Dagueneau; and from Alsace there are enough Zind-Humbrecht wines to sink a ship. Interesting French wines also come from Provence (Ch. de Pibarnon) and the Rhône (Alain Graillot). Increasing coverage of South Africa.*

D Byrne & Co

Victoria Buildings, 12 King Street, Clitheroe, Lancs BB7 2EP (01200) 423152 HOURS Mon–Sat 8.30–6 CARDS MasterCard, Switch, Visa DELIVERY Free within 50 miles; nationally £10 1st case, £5 subsequent cases EN PRIMEUR Bordeaux, Burgundy, Rhône, Germany. **G M T**
✪ **Star attractions** *One of northern England's best wine merchants, with a hugely impressive range. Clarets back to 1978, stacks of Burgundy, faultless Loire and Rhône, Germany, Spain, USA (not just California) and many, many more. I urge you to go and see for yourself.*

Cape Wine and Food

77 Laleham Road, Staines, Middx TW18 2EA (01784) 451860 FAX (01784) 469267 E-MAIL capewineandfood@aol.com WEBSITE www.capewinestores.co.uk HOURS Mon–Sat 10–6 CARDS MasterCard, Switch, Visa DISCOUNTS 10% on 12 bottles DELIVERY £6.95 per case. **G M T**
✪ **Star attractions** *South African wines, many from top names such as Graham Beck, Iona, Thelema and Vergelegen.*

Cave Cru Classé

MAIL ORDER Unit 13 The
Leathermarket, Weston Street,
London SE1 3ER (020) 7378 8579
FAX (020) 7378 8544 and 7403 0607
E-MAIL enquiries@ccc.co.uk
WEBSITE www.cave-cru-classe.com
HOURS Mon–Fri 9–5.30 **CARDS**
AmEx, MasterCard, Visa **DELIVERY**
£20 per order in London and the
South-East; at cost elsewhere
MINIMUM ORDER 1 mixed case
EN PRIMEUR Bordeaux. **M T**
✪ Star attractions *1945 was an
excellent vintage for red Bordeaux,
and if you'd like to splash out for
a friend's sixtieth birthday Cave
Cru Classé have a selection of
excellent clarets, ranging from
£150 to £995, plus VAT. If Burgundy
or Rhône are your wines of choice,
there are pages of top names to
choose from. Italy and port look
starry, too.*

Les Caves de Pyrene

Pew Corner, Old Portsmouth Road,
Artington, Guildford GU3 1LP
(office) (01483) 538820 (shop)
(01483) 554750 **FAX** (01483) 455068
E-MAIL sales@lescaves.co.uk
WEBSITE www.lescaves.co.uk **HOURS**
(office) Mon–Sat 9–5 (shop)
Mon–Sat 9–7 **CARDS** MasterCard,
Switch, Visa **DELIVERY** Free for
orders over £200 within M25,
elsewhere at cost **DISCOUNTS**
negotiable **MINIMUM ORDER**
1 mixed case **EN PRIMEUR**
South-West France. **G M T**
✪ Star attractions *Excellent
operation, devoted to seeking out
top wines from all over southern
France. Other areas of France,
especially the Loire, are equally
good. And there's Armagnac dating
back to 1893!*

ChateauOnline

MAIL ORDER 29 rue Ganneron,
75018 Paris (0033) 1 55 30 31 41
FAX (0033) 1 55 30 31 41 **CUSTOMER
SERVICE** 0800 169 2736 **WEBSITE**
www.chateauonline.com **HOURS**
Mon–Fri 8–11.30, 12.30–4.30 **CARDS**
AmEx, MasterCard, Switch, Visa
DELIVERY £7.99 per consignment
EN PRIMEUR Bordeaux, Burgundy,
Languedoc-Roussillon.
✪ Star attractions *French specialist,
with an impressive list of over 3,000
wines. Easy-to-use website with a
well-thought-out range of mixed
cases, frequent special offers and
bin end sales.*

Cockburns of Leith (incorporating J E Hogg)

The Wine Emporium, 7 Devon
Place, Haymarket, Edinburgh EH12
5HJ (0131) 346 1113 **FAX** (0131) 313
2607 **E-MAIL** sales@winelist.co.uk
WEBSITE www.winelist.co.uk
HOURS Mon–Fri 9–6; Sat 10–5
CARDS MasterCard, Switch, Visa
DELIVERY Free 12 or more bottles
within Edinburgh; elsewhere
£7 1–2 cases, free 3 cases or more
EN PRIMEUR Bordeaux, Burgundy. **G T**
✪ Star attractions *Clarets at
bargain prices, Burgundies from
Champy – in fact wines from all
over France, including plenty of
vins de pays. There are also well-
chosen wines from Italy, Chile,
Argentina, South Africa and New
Zealand.*

Connolly's Wine Merchants

Arch 13, 220 Livery Street,
Birmingham B3 1EU (0121) 236
9269/3837 **FAX** (0121) 233 2339
E-MAIL sales@connollyswine.co.uk
WEBSITE www.connollyswine.co.uk
HOURS Mon–Fri 9–5.30, Sat 10–4
CARDS AmEx, MasterCard, Switch,
Visa **DELIVERY** Surcharge outside
Birmingham area **DISCOUNTS** 10%
for cash & carry **EN PRIMEUR**
Bordeaux, Burgundy, Port. **G M T**
✪ Star attractions *Bordeaux,
Burgundy and the Rhône all look
very good; a short German list
includes Dr Loosen; Italy has names
like Isole e Olena and Allegrini; and
from Spain there are Riojas from*

Faustino and Artadi. Fizz includes
Pirie from Tasmania and Pelorus
from New Zealand.

The Co-operative Group

HEAD OFFICE New Century House,
Manchester M60 4ES, freephone
0800 068 6727 for stock details
FAX (0161) 827 5117; approx. 3,000
licensed stores **E-MAIL** customer
relations@co-op.co.uk **WEBSITE**
www.co-op.co.uk **HOURS** Variable
CARDS Variable • **ONLINE WINE STORE**
www.co-opdrinks2u.com **TELEPHONE**
0845 090 2222 **CARDS** AmEx,
MasterCard, Solo, Switch, Visa
DELIVERY Within 7 days mainland UK
£4.99 (UK islands and N. Ireland

£23); Saturday delivery (major
towns only) £26 **MINIMUM ORDER**
Wine sold in multiples of 3, can be
mixed.
✪ **Star attractions** *Champions of
English, organic and Fairtrade
wines, and good modern wines
from Cyprus under the Island
Vines and Mountain Vines labels.
Plenty of good stuff for less than
a fiver.*

Corney & Barrow

HEAD OFFICE No. 1 Thomas More
Street, London EC1V 3TD (020) 7265
2400 **FAX** (020) 7265 2539
• 194 Kensington Park Road, London
W11 2ES (020) 7221 5122

Retailers directory

• Corney & Barrow East Anglia, Belvoir House, High Street, Newmarket CB8 8DH (01638) 600000 • Corney & Barrow (Scotland) with Whighams of Ayr, 8 Academy Street, Ayr KA7 1HT (01292) 267000, and Oxenfoord Castle, by Pathhead, Mid Lothian, EH37 5UD (01875) 321921 E-MAIL wine@corbar.co.uk WEBSITE www.corneyand barrow.com HOURS Mon–Fri 9–6 (24-hr answering machine); Kensington Mon–Fri 10.30–9, Sat 9.30–8; Newmarket Mon–Sat 9–6; Edinburgh Mon–Fri 9–6; Ayr Mon–Fri 9–6, Sat 9.30–5.30 CARDS AmEx, MasterCard, Switch, Visa DELIVERY Free 2 or more cases within M25 boundary, elsewhere free 3 or more cases or for orders above £200. Otherwise £9 + VAT per delivery. For Scotland and East Anglia, please contact the relevant office EN PRIMEUR Bordeaux, Burgundy, Champagne, Italy, Spain, South America, USA. **C G M T**
✪ Star attractions *If you want certain Pomerols like Pétrus, Trotanoy, la Fleur-Pétrus and Latour à Pomerol, Corney & Barrow, by Royal Appointment, is where you have to come. At least, if you want them en primeur. Burgundy kicks off with Domaine de la Romanée-Conti and proceeds via names like Domaine Trapet and Domaine Leflaive. The rest of Europe is equally impressive; while there is good stuff from the New World, there's less of it.*

Croque-en-Bouche
221 Wells Road, Malvern Wells, Worcestershire WR14 4HF (01684) 565612 FAX (08707) 066282 E-MAIL mail@croque-en-bouche.co.uk WEBSITE www.croque-en-bouche. co.uk HOURS By appointment 7 days a week CARDS MasterCard, Switch, Visa DISCOUNTS 3% for orders over £500 if paid in cash or by Switch or Delta, 1.5% if paid by credit card

DELIVERY Free locally; elsewhere £5 per consignment MINIMUM ORDER 1 mixed case. **M**
✪ Star attractions *A wonderful list, including older wines. Mature Australian reds from the 1990s; terrific stuff from the Rhône – Château Beaucastel's Châteauneuf-du-Pape going back to 1979; some top clarets (1961 Ch. Léoville-Barton for £200) and from Alsace, loads of Zind-Humbrecht; and a generous sprinkling from other parts of the world. Sweet wines include mature Sauternes and Loire wines from the great '47 vintage.*

Devigne Wines
Mas Y Coed, 13 Llanerchydol Park, Welshpool SY21 9QE (01938) 553478 FAX (01938) 556831 E-MAIL info@devignewines.co.uk WEBSITE www.devignewines.co.uk HOURS Mon–Fri 10–6 (telephone 7 days) CARDS MasterCard, Switch, Visa DISCOUNTS selected mixed cases at introductory rate DELIVERY free for orders over £300, otherwise £6.50 per consignment MINIMUM ORDER 1 mixed case. **M**
✪ Star attractions *Small list specializing in French wines: 14 different rosés and 19 traditional-(Champagne) method sparkling wines from all over France as well as red Gaillac from the South-West and some lovely Languedoc reds.*

Direct Wine Shipments
5–7 Corporation Square, Belfast, N Ireland BT1 3AJ (028) 9050 8000 FAX (028) 9050 8004 E-MAIL shop@directwine.co.uk WEBSITE www.directwine.co.uk HOURS Mon–Fri 9–6.30 (Thur 10–8), Sat 9.30–5.30 CARDS MasterCard, Switch, Visa DISCOUNTS 10% in the form of complimentary wine with each case DELIVERY Free N Ireland 1 case or more, variable delivery charge for UK mainland depending on customer spend EN PRIMEUR Bordeaux, Rhône. **C M T**

✪ **Star attractions** *Rhône, Spain, Australia and Burgundy look outstanding, Italy and Germany are not far behind, and from Chile there's Santa Rita and Miguel Torres. In fact there's good stuff from pretty well everywhere.*

Dodici

PO Box 428, Harpenden, Hertfordshire AL5 3ZT (01582) 713004 FAX (01582) 767991 E-MAIL angus@dodici.co.uk WEBSITE www.dodici.co.uk HOURS Mon–Fri 9–6.30 (Thur 10–8), Sat 9.30–5.30 CARDS MasterCard, Switch, Visa DELIVERY Free locally. M T
✪ **Star attractions** *There's such a wealth of interesting wine in Italy that it's really encouraging to find an independent company seeking out jewels that are usually hidden to the British consumer. Choose a pre-mixed case or create your own from a terrific list that includes plenty of wines at £6–7.*

Domaine Direct

3 Cynthia Street, London N1 9JF (020) 7837 1142 FAX (020) 7837 3605 E-MAIL mail@domainedirect.co.uk WEBSITE www.domainedirect.co.uk HOURS 8.30–6 or answering machine CARDS MasterCard, Switch, Visa DELIVERY Free London; elsewhere in UK mainland 1 case £11.50, 2 cases £15, 3 or more free MINIMUM ORDER 1 mixed case EN PRIMEUR Burgundy. M T
✪ **Star attractions** *Sensational Burgundy list. From Australia you'll find wines from the Leeuwin Estate; from California there's Etude, Nalle, Paradigm and Spottswoode.*

Farr Vintners

20 Queenstown Road, Battersea, London SW8 4LP (020) 7821 2000 FAX (020) 7821 2020 E-MAIL sales@farrvintners.com WEBSITE www.farrvintners.com HOURS Mon–Fri 10–6 CARDS Switch

DELIVERY London £1 per case (min £14); elsewhere at cost MINIMUM ORDER £500 + VAT EN PRIMEUR Bordeaux. C M
✪ **Star attractions** *A fantastic list of the world's finest wines. The majority is Bordeaux, but you'll also find top stuff and older vintages from Burgundy, the Rhône, Italy (Gaja, Sassicaia), Australia and California (Araujo, Dominus).*

Irma Fingal-Rock

64 Monnow Street, Monmouth NP25 3EN TEL & FAX 01600 712372 E-MAIL tom@pinotnoir.co.uk WEBSITE www.pinotnoir.co.uk HOURS Mon 9.30–1.30, Thurs & Fri 9.30–5.30, Sat 9.30–5 CARDS MasterCard, Switch, Visa DISCOUNTS 5% for at least 12 bottles collected from shop, 7.5% for collected orders over £500, 10% for collected orders over £1,200 DELIVERY Free locally (within 30 miles); orders further afield free if over £100. G M T
✪ **Star attractions** *The list's great strength is Burgundy, from some very good growers and priced between £6 and £34. Small but tempting selections from Bordeaux, Loire, Rhône and other French regions. Ditto Italy, Spain, Portugal and the New World. Two local (yes, Welsh) producers are also represented.*

Flagship Wines

417 Hatfield Road, St Albans, Hertfordshire AL4 0XP TEL & FAX (01727) 841968 E-MAIL info@flagshipwines.co.uk WEBSITE www.flagshipwines.co.uk HOURS 10–6 Mon–Sat CARDS MasterCard, Switch, Visa DELIVERY Free within 20 miles of St Albans; £7.50 per case elsewhere in UK mainland. G M T
✪ **Star attractions** *Well-run independent whose prices can match those of the supermarkets – and you get the friendly, well-*

informed advice of boss Julia Jenkins thrown in for free. Good Chilean and French basics, interesting Italians, and strongest in Spain and Australia.

Le Fleming Wines

MAIL ORDER 19 Spenser Road, Harpenden, Hertfordshire AL5 5NW (01582) 760125 **E-MAIL** cherry@leflemingwines.co.uk **WEBSITE** www.leflemingwines.co.uk **HOURS** 24-hour answering machine **DISCOUNTS** 5% on large orders **DELIVERY** Free locally **MINIMUM ORDER** 1 case. **G**

✪ Star attractions Australia looks terrific here, with lots of serious and not so serious wines. South Africa, too, is good, with wines from Hamilton Russell and Thelema. The list is basically the New World and France, plus short but focused selections from Italy and Spain.

The Flying Corkscrew

Leighton Buzzard Road, Water End, Nr Hemel Hempstead, Hertfordshire HP1 3BD (01442) 412311 **FAX** (01442) 412313 **E-MAIL** sales@flyingcorkscrew.com **WEBSITE** www.flyingcorkscrew.com **HOURS** Mon–Wed 10–8, Thurs–Fri 10–9, Sat 10–7, Sun 11–5 **CARDS** AmEx, MasterCard, Switch, Visa **DISCOUNTS** 10% on case **DELIVERY** Free locally, £15 per case UK mainland. **G M T**

✪ Star attractions A very stylish shop with friendly, knowledgable staff and an extensive and imaginative range of wines. If you're local, look out for tastings led by experts and winemakers such as Randall Grahm of Bonny Doon, and Douro specialist Dirk Niepoort.

Fortnum & Mason

181 Piccadilly, London W1A 1ER (020) 7734 8040 **FAX** (020) 7437 3278 **ORDERING LINE** 0845 300 1707 **E-MAIL** info@fortnumandmason. co.uk **WEBSITE** www.fortnumand mason.co.uk **HOURS** Mon–Sat 10–6.30, Sun 12–6 (Food Hall and Patio Restaurant only) **CARDS** AmEx, Diners, MasterCard, Switch, Visa **DISCOUNTS** 1 free bottle per unmixed dozen **DELIVERY** £6 per delivery address **EN PRIMEUR** Bordeaux. **M T**

✪ Star attractions Champagne, Bordeaux and Burgundy are the leaders of a very smart pack, but there are names to impress from just about everywhere, including the cream of the crop from Italy, Germany, Australia, New Zealand, South Africa and California. Impeccably sourced own-label range.

Friarwood

26 New King's Road, London SW6 4ST (020) 7736 2628 **FAX** (020) 7731 0411 • 16 Dock Street, Leith, Edinburgh EH6 6EY (0131) 554 4159 **FAX** (0131) 554 6703 **E-MAIL** sales@friarwood.com; edinburgh@friarwood.com **WEBSITE** www.friarwood.com **HOURS** Mon–Sat 10–7 **CARDS** AmEx, Diners, MasterCard, Switch, Visa, Solo, Electron **DISCOUNTS** 5% on mixed cases, 10% unmixed **DELIVERY** (London) Free within M25 and on orders over £250 in mainland UK (Edinburgh) free locally and for 2 cases or more elsewhere (under 2 cases at cost) **EN PRIMEUR** Bordeaux, Burgundy. **C G M T**

✪ Star attractions The focus is Bordeaux, including a good selection of petits châteaux as well as classed growths; vintages available go back to 1982, or 1967 for Yquem. Burgundy is mostly from Domaine Antonin Guyon. New wines from Italy, some good Californians, Magnotta icewine from Canada and a wide range of Armagnacs round off this imaginative list.

Gauntleys

4 High Street, Exchange Arcade, Nottingham NG1 2ET (0115)

911 0555 **FAX** (0115) 911 0557
E-MAIL rhone@gauntleywine.com
WEBSITE www.gauntleywine.com
HOURS Mon–Sat 9–5.30 **CARDS**
MasterCard, Switch, Visa **DELIVERY**
Free within Nottingham area,
otherwise 1–3 cases £9.50, 4 or
more cases free **MINIMUM ORDER** 1
case **EN PRIMEUR** Alsace, Burgundy,
Italy, Loire, Rhône, southern France,
Spain. **M T**
✪ **Star attractions** *They've won
awards for their Rhône list, but it
doesn't stop there: Alsace, Loire,
Burgundy, southern France, Spain
and Italy are all top-notch. No
Bordeaux. Champagne is Vilmart's
wonderfully big, rich wines.*

Goedhuis & Co

6 Rudolf Place, Miles Street,
London SW8 1RP (020) 7793
7900 **FAX** (020) 7793 7170
E-MAIL sales@goedhuis.com
WEBSITE www.goedhuis.com
HOURS Mon–Fri 9–5.30 **CARDS**
AmEx, MasterCard, Switch, Visa
DELIVERY Free 3 cases or more,
otherwise £10 England, elsewhere
at cost **MINIMUM ORDER** 1 unmixed
case **EN PRIMEUR** Bordeaux,
Burgundy. **C G M T**
✪ **Star attractions** *Fine wine
specialist. Bordeaux, Burgundy and
fine Italian wines are the core of the
list, but everything is good, and if
you buy your everyday wines here
you'll get very good quality, plus
friendly, expert advice.*

Great Northern Wine

The Warehouse, Blossomgate,
Ripon, N. Yorks HG4 2AJ (01765)
606767 **FAX** (01765) 609151
E-MAIL info@greatnorthern
wine.com **HOURS** Mon–Fri 9–6, Sat
9–5.30 **CARDS** AmEx, MasterCard,
Switch, Visa **DISCOUNTS** 10% on case
quantities **DELIVERY** Free locally,
elsewhere at cost. **G M T**
✪ **Star attractions** *A sound list that
mixes well-known and less familiar
names: Australia (Campbells,*

The Oz Clarke
Wine Collection
Buy direct, at a discount, on
www.ozclarke.com

Oz's Awards

Oz Clarke has won all the major wine-writing awards both in the UK and USA, including the Glenfiddich (three times), André Simon, Wine Guild (three times), James Beard, Julia Child, Lanson (six times) and World Food Media (twice). His far-reaching influence on the modern world of wine was publicly acknowledge when he won the Lanson Special Millennium Award for his outstanding contribution to wine communication and education. Most recently C *Clarke's Pocket Wine Book 2004* won the Prix Lanson Wine Guide of the Year award.

Everything you need to know about wine from
THE WINE MAN

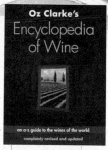

Tyrrell's), New Zealand (Alpha Domus, Trinity Hill), Portugal and Spain look terrific. France looks highly desirable too.

Great Western Wine

The Wine Warehouse, Wells Road, Bath BA2 3AP (01225) 322810 FAX (01225) 442139 E-MAIL retail@greatwesternwine.co.uk WEBSITE www.greatwestern wine.co.uk HOURS Mon–Fri 10–7, Sat 10–6 CARDS AmEx, MasterCard, Switch, Visa DISCOUNTS Negotiable DELIVERY Free 3 or more cases, otherwise £6 MINIMUM ORDER 1 mixed case EN PRIMEUR Australia, Bordeaux, Burgundy, Rhône, Spain. C G M T

✪ Star attractions *Great Western bring in wines from individual growers around the world. Highlights include Bonnefond and Gilles Robin from the Rhône, Glaetzer, Heartland and Ferngrove from Australia.*

Peter Green & Co

37A/B Warrender Park Road, Edinburgh EH9 1HJ TEL & FAX (0131) 229 5925 HOURS Tues–Thur 10–6.30, Fri 10–7.30, Sat 10–6.30 CARDS MasterCard, Switch, Visa DISCOUNTS 5% on unmixed half-dozens DELIVERY Free in Edinburgh MINIMUM ORDER (For delivery) 1 case. G T

✪ Star attractions *Extensive, well-chosen and adventurous list from all over the world.*

Roger Harris Wines

Loke Farm, Weston Longville, Norfolk NR9 5LG (01603) 880171 FAX (01603) 880291 E-MAIL sales@rogerharriswines.co.uk WEBSITE www.rogerharris wines.co.uk HOURS Mon–Fri 9–5 CARDS AmEx, MasterCard, Visa DELIVERY next working day UK mainland, £3 for orders up to £110, £2 up to £160, free over £160 MINIMUM ORDER 1 mixed case. M

✪ Star attractions *Beaujolais-loving family business – Britain's acknowledged experts in this area. The list also ventures into the Mâconnais, Champagne and the south of France. Now includes small producers from Australia and South Africa.*

Harvey Nichols

109–125 Knightsbridge, London SW1X 7RJ (020) 7235 5000 • The Mailbox, 31–32 Wharfside Street, Birmingham B1 1RE (0121) 616 6000 • 30–34 St Andrew Square, Edinburgh EH2 3AD (0131) 524 8388 • 107–111 Briggate, Leeds LS1 6AZ (0113) 204 8888 • 21 New Cathedral Street, Manchester M3 1RE (0161) 828 8888 E-MAIL wineshop@ harveynichols.com WEBSITE www.harveynichols.com HOURS (London) Mon–Fri 10–8, Sat 10–7, Sun 12–6 (Birmingham) Mon-Wed 10–6, Thurs 10–8, Fri–Sat 10–7, Sun 11–5 (Edinburgh) Mon–Wed 10–6, Thurs 10–8, Fri, Sat 10–7, Sun 11–5 (Leeds) Mon–Wed 10–6, Thurs–Fri 10–7, Sat 9–7, Sun 12–6 (Manchester) Mon, Wed, Fri 10–7, Thurs 10–8, Sat 9–7, Sun 12–6 CARDS AmEx, MasterCard, Switch, Visa.

✪ Star attractions *Top names from France, Italy and California, especially for sought-after producers such as Harlan, Kistler and Turley.*

Haynes Hanson & Clark

Sheep Street, Stow-on-the-Wold, Glos GL54 1AA (01451) 870808 FAX (01451) 870508 • 25 Eccleston Street, London SW1W 9NP (020) 7259 0102 FAX (020) 7259 0103 E-MAIL stow@hhandc.co.uk or london@hhandc.co.uk HOURS (Stow) Mon–Fri 9–6, Sat 9–5.30 (London) Mon–Fri 9–7 CARDS AmEx, MasterCard, Switch, Visa DISCOUNTS 10% unsplit case DELIVERY Free central London and Glos; elsewhere 1 case £8, 2–3 cases

£12.45 per case, 4 or more cases £10.15 per case, free orders over £650 **EN PRIMEUR** Bordeaux, Burgundy, Rhône. **G M T**
✪ **Star attractions** *HH&C's preference is for subtle, elegant wines, so you won't find too many hefty blockbusters here. It's most famous for Burgundy – but there are also lovely wines from the Loire, Alsace and Rhône, Germany, Australia, New Zealand and California. Bordeaux is chosen to suit every pocket. Their house Champagne, Pierre Vaudon, is invariably a winner.*

Hedley Wright

11 Twyford Centre, London Road, Bishop's Stortford, Herts CM23 3YT (01279) 465818 **FAX** (01279) 465819 **E-MAIL** sales@hedleywright.co.uk **WEBSITE** www.hedleywright.co.uk **HOURS** Mon–Wed 9–6, Thur–Fri 9–7, Sat 10–6 **CARDS** AmEx, MasterCard, Switch, Visa **DELIVERY** £5 per delivery, free for orders over £100 **MINIMUM ORDER** 1 mixed case **EN PRIMEUR** Bordeaux, Chile, Germany, Port. **C G M T**
✪ **Star attractions** *A good all-round list that does justice to most French regions. Italy, something of a speciality, has wines from the likes of Pieropan, Allegrini and Le Pupille. Portugal, Spain, South Africa, New Zealand and Australia are packed with interesting wines, and Chile majors on the wines of Montes.*

Hicks & Don

4 Old Station Yard, Edington, Westbury, Wiltshire BA13 4NT (01380) 831234 **FAX** (01380) 831010 • Park House, North Elmham, Dereham, Norfolk NR20 5JY (01362) 668571 **FAX** (01362) 668573 **E-MAIL** mailbox@hicksanddon.co.uk **WEBSITE** www.hicksanddon.co.uk **HOURS** Mon–Fri 9–5 **CARDS** MasterCard, Switch, Visa **DISCOUNTS** Negotiable **DELIVERY** Free 3 cases or

more UK mainland, otherwise £6 per case **MINIMUM ORDER** 1 case **EN PRIMEUR** Bordeaux, Burgundy, Chile, Italy, Port, Rhône. **C G M T**
✪ **Star attractions** *Subtle, well-made wines that go with food and plenty of good-value wines at around £6 for everyday drinking. The list is set out by style, regardless of origin: white Burgundies and other Chardonnays are followed by Sauvignons and Sémillons, then 'white wines of individuality' – the likes of Vin de Pays des Côtes de Gascogne, Muscadet and Pieropan's Soave Classico – then dessert wines, then Rieslings.*

High Breck Vintners

MAIL ORDER 11 Nelson Road, London N8 9RX (020) 8340 1848 **FAX** (020) 8340 5162 **E-MAIL** hbv@richanl.freeserve.co.uk **WEBSITE** www.hbvwines.co.uk **HOURS** Mail order only; 24-hr answering machine for orders **CARDS** AmEx, MasterCard, Switch, Visa **DELIVERY** Free to the South-East, 3 or more cases; supplements payable for smaller orders or other locations **MINIMUM ORDER** 1 mixed case **EN PRIMEUR** Bordeaux. **C G M T**
✪ **Star attractions** *A shortish list with the focus on France, especially Bordeaux. Madiran is from Alain Brumont, Sancerre from Gitton Père et Fils. Wines from lesser-known appellations like Costières de Nîmes can provide good drinking at lower prices. A sprinkling of good names from Spain, Italy and Australia.*

Jeroboams (incorporating Laytons)

HEAD OFFICE 43 Portland Road, London W11 4LJ (020) 7985 1560 **FAX** (020) 7229 1085 **MAIL ORDER** Jeroboams, 6 Pont Street, London SW1X 9EL (020) 7259 6716 **FAX** (020) 7235 7246 **SHOPS** 50–52 Elizabeth Street, London SW1W 9PB (020) 7730 8108 • 51 Elizabeth Street, London SW1W 9PP

Retailers directory

(020) 7823 5623 • 20 Davies Street,
London W1K 3DT (020) 7499 1015
• 77–78 Chancery Lane, London
WC2A 1AE (020) 7405 0552
• 96 Holland Park Avenue, London
W11 3RB (020) 7727 9359 • 6 Pont
Street, London SW1X 9EL (020) 7235
1612 • 3 The Market Place,
Cirencester, Glos GL7 2PE
(01285) 655842 • Mr Christian's
Delicatessen, 11 Elgin Crescent,
London W11 2JA, (020) 7229 0501
E-MAIL sales@jeroboams.co.uk
WEBSITES www.jeroboams.co.uk
HOURS Offices Mon–Fri 9–6, shops
Mon–Sat 9–7 (may vary) CARDS
AmEx, MasterCard, Switch, Visa
DELIVERY Shops: free for orders of
£50 or over in central London; mail
order free for orders over £200,
otherwise £10 delivery charge
EN PRIMEUR Bordeaux, Burgundy,
Rhône. C G M T
✪ Star attractions *Sensibly priced
everyday clarets as well as classed
growths, interesting Burgundies and
a good list from the Rhône. Other
regions of France – including Jura –
are covered though in less depth.
Italy and Australia – in particular
Western Australia – are new
specialities. A wide range of fine
foods, especially cheeses and olive
oils, is available in the shops.*

S H Jones

27 High Street, Banbury,
Oxfordshire OX16 5EW (01295)
251179 FAX (01295) 272352
• 9 Market Square, Bicester,
Oxfordshire OX26 6AA (01869)
322448 • The Cellar Shop, 2
Riverside Tramway Road, Banbury,
Oxfordshire OX16 5TU (01295)
251177 FAX (01295) 259560 • 121
Regent Street, Leamington Spa,
Warwickshire CV32 4NU (01926)
315609 E-MAIL retail@shjones.com
WEBSITE www.shjones.com
HOURS Mon–Sat 8.30–6 CARDS
MasterCard, Switch, Visa DELIVERY
Free within van delivery area for
1 case or more; 'small charge'

otherwise. Elsewhere £7.50; free
for orders over £250 EN PRIMEUR
Bordeaux, Burgundy, Port. C G M T
✪ Star attractions *Wide-ranging
list: good Burgundies and Rhônes;
some top-name clarets, along with
'everyday' ones at around £10; and a
comprehensive and affordable
selection from southern France.
Other good stuff from Old and New
World includes Dr Loosen from
Germany and Terrazas de los Andes
from Argentina.*

Justerini & Brooks

MAIL ORDER 61 St James's Street,
London SW1A 1LZ (020) 7484 6400
FAX (020) 7484 6499 E-MAIL
justorders@justerinis.com
WEBSITE www.justerinis.com
HOURS Mon–Fri 9–5.30 CARDS
AmEx, MasterCard, Switch, Visa
DELIVERY Free for orders over £250,
otherwise £15 UK mainland
MINIMUM ORDER 1 case EN PRIMEUR
Bordeaux, Burgundy, Italy, Rhône.
C G M T
✪ Star attractions *Superb list of
top-quality wines from Europe's
classic regions. The New World,
though succinct, also has some
excellent drinking. And while there
are some very classy – and pricy –
wines here, you'll find plenty of
bottles under £7.*

Kwiksave
See Somerfield.

Laithwaites

MAIL ORDER New Aquitaine House,
Exeter Way, Theale, Reading, Berks
RG7 4PL; ORDER LINE 0870 444 8383
FAX 0870 444 8182 E-MAIL
orders@laithwaites.co.uk
WEBSITE www.laithwaites.co.uk
HOURS 24-hr answering machine
CARDS AmEx, Diners, MasterCard,
Switch, Visa DISCOUNTS On unmixed
cases of 6 or 12 DELIVERY £4.99
per order EN PRIMEUR Australia,
Bordeaux, Burgundy, Port, Rhône,
Rioja. C M T

✪ **Star attractions** *Good selection including well-known names and interesting finds. The lists are generally the same as those for the Sunday Times Wine Club although some wines are exclusive to each. User-friendly website offers excellent mixed cases, while the bin ends and special offers are good value. Added extras include wine plans offering regular delivery of hand-picked cases, and a comprehensive database for matching wine and food – from cold fresh prawns to kangeroo steaks!*

The Lay & Wheeler Group

Holton Park, Holston St Mary, Suffolk CO7 6NN 0845 330 1855 **FAX** 0845 330 4095 **E-MAIL** sales@laywheeler. com **WEBSITE** www.laywheeler.com **HOURS** (order office) Mon–Fri 8.30–5.30, Sat 8.30–1 **CARDS** AmEx, MasterCard, Switch, Visa **DELIVERY** £7.95; free for orders over £150 **EN PRIMEUR** Alsace, Australia, Bordeaux, Burgundy, California, Champagne, Germany, Italy, Loire, Rhône, Spain. **C G M T**

✪ **Star attractions** *There's enough first-class Bordeaux and Burgundy to satisfy the most demanding drinker here; indeed everything is excellent. A must-have list – and if you really can't make up your mind, their mixed cases are excellent too.*

Laymont & Shaw

The Old Chapel, Millpool, Truro, Cornwall TR1 1EX (01872) 270545 **FAX** (01872) 223005 **E-MAIL** info@laymont-shaw.co.uk **WEBSITE** www.laymont-shaw.co.uk **HOURS** Mon–Fri 9–5 **CARDS** MasterCard, Switch, Visa **DISCOUNTS** £5 per case if wines collected, also £1 per case for 2 cases, £2 for 3–5, £3 for 6 or more **DELIVERY** Free UK mainland **MINIMUM ORDER** 1 mixed case. **C G M T**

✪ **Star attractions** *An excellent, knowledgeable list that specializes in Spain, with Portugal and Uruguay also featuring. And when I say 'specializes', I mean that they seek out wines that you won't find in supermarkets because the quantities are too small.*

Laytons

See Jeroboams.

Lea & Sandeman

170 Fulham Road, London SW10 9PR (020) 7244 0522 **FAX** (020) 7244 0533 • 211 Kensington Church Street, London W8 7LX (020) 7221 1982 • 51 High Street, Barnes, London SW13 9LN (020) 8878 8643 **E-MAIL** info@leaandsandeman.co.uk **WEBSITE** www.londonfinewine.co.uk **HOURS** Mon–Sat 10–8 **CARDS** AmEx, MasterCard, Switch, Visa **DISCOUNTS** 5–15% by case, other discounts on 10 cases or more **DELIVERY** £5 for less than 1 case; free 1 case or more London, and to UK mainland south of Perth on orders over £250 **EN PRIMEUR** Bordeaux, Burgundy, Italy. **C G M T**

✪ **Star attractions** *Burgundy and Italy take precedence here, and there's a succession of excellent names, chosen with great care. But L&S really do seek out unknown treasures wherever they go, so it's worth taking the time to study the list carefully. Bordeaux has wines at all price levels, and there are short but fascinating ranges from the US, Spain, Australia, New Zealand and South Africa.*

Liberty Wines

MAIL ORDER Unit D18, New Covent Garden Food Market, London SW8 5LL (020) 7720 5350 **FAX** (020) 7720 6158 **E-MAIL** info@libertywine.co.uk **HOURS** Mon–Fri 9–5.30 **CARDS** MasterCard, Switch, Visa **DELIVERY**

Come and *taste* the Majestic experience

NATIONWIDE STORES
115 stores across the UK, open 7 days a week

100s OF WINES ON SPECIAL OFFER

FREE HOME DELIVERY
Of a mixed case of wine *anywhere* in mainland U

FINE WINES
Latest list available at
www.majestic.co.uk/finewine

AWARD WINNING SERVICE
From friendly, knowledgeable staff

FREE TASTING
Wines open to taste, all day, every day

ORDER ONLINE
Visit Majestic Online www.majestic.co.uk
E-mail us at info@majestic.co.uk

* We're sorry that this excludes the Scottish Islands, Northern Ireland, Isles of Scilly and the Isle of Man. Mail order deliveries to these locations can be arranged for a nominal charge. Please call our Mail Order department on 01727 847935 for further information. We do not deliver to the Channel Islands and destinations outside of the UK.

www.majestic.co.

Visiting France?
Wine & Beer World is Majestic Wine Warehouses French operation offering the best value wines in the Channel ports. Wines start from only 99p and include many Majestic favourites. With more than 100 products on Special Offer you can expect to save up to 50% on the UK price of your drinks bill. We offer a pre-ordering servic free tasting and a friendly, knowledgeable English speaking service.

Please call 01923 298297 or visit
www.wineandbeer.co.uk
for a free price list and
directions to our stores in Calais,
Coquelles and Cherbourg.

Free to mainland UK **MINIMUM ORDER** 1 mixed case. **M**
✪ Star attractions *Italy rules, with superb wines and pretty well all the best producers from all over the country. Liberty are the UK agents for most of their producers, so if you're interested in Italian wines, this should be your first port of call. California features producers like Seghesio and Testarossa, and from Australia there's Cullen, Mount Horrocks, Charles Melton and Plantagenet. France, Germany and South America are not neglected.*

O W Loeb & Co

3 Archie Street, off Tanner Street, London SE1 3JT (020) 7234 0385 **FAX** (020) 7357 0440 **E-MAIL** finewine@owloeb.com **WEBSITE** www.owloeb.com **HOURS** Mon–Fri 8.30–5.30 **CARDS** MasterCard, Switch, Visa **DISCOUNTS** 5 cases and above **DELIVERY** Free 2 cases or more **MINIMUM ORDER** 1 case **EN PRIMEUR** Burgundy, Rhône, Germany (Mosel), Bordeaux. **C M T**
✪ Star attractions *Burgundy, the Rhône, Loire and Germany stand out, with top producers galore. Then there are Loeb's new discoveries from Spain and the New World, especially New Zealand and South Africa.*

Majestic

(see also Wine and Beer World)
HEAD OFFICE Majestic House, Otterspool Way, Watford, Herts WD25 8WW (01923) 298200 **FAX** (01923) 819105; 115 stores nationwide **E-MAIL** info@majestic. co.uk **WEBSITE** www.majestic.co.uk **HOURS** Mon–Fri 10–8, Sat 9–7, Sun 10–5 (may vary) **CARDS** AmEx, Diners, MasterCard, Switch, Visa **DELIVERY** Free UK mainland **MINIMUM ORDER** 1 mixed case **EN PRIMEUR** Bordeaux, Port. **G M T**
✪ Star attractions *This has long been one of the best places to come for Champagne, with a good range and good discounts for buying in*

quantity. Elsewhere you'll find real stars rubbing shoulders with some interesting oddballs. The Loire and Alsace are good, as are Germany, Italy and most of the New World.*

Marks & Spencer

HEAD OFFICE Waterside House, 35 North Wharf Road, London W2 1NW (020) 7935 4422 **FAX** (020) 7723 4924; 350 licensed stores **WEBSITE** www.marksandspencer.com **HOURS** Variable **DISCOUNTS** Variable, Wine of the Month, 12 bottles for the price of 11. **T**
✪ Star attractions *M&S source their wines from top producers, so you can't go far wrong: they've found some terrific stuff from Australia, and the Shepherds Ridge Sauvignon Blanc is made by one of New Zealand's hottest young winemakers, Brent Marris, the man behind Wither Hills. Their Spanish range is looking particularly good this year.*

Martinez Wines

35 The Grove, Ilkley, Leeds, W. Yorks LS29 9NJ (01943) 603241 **FAX** 0870 922 3940 **E-MAIL** editor@martinez. co.uk **WEBSITE** www.martinez.co.uk **HOURS** Mon–Wed 10–6, Thurs–Fri 10–8, Sat 9.30–6 **CARDS** AmEx, MasterCard, Switch, Visa **DISCOUNTS** 5% on 6 bottles or more, 10% off orders over £150 **DELIVERY** Free local delivery, otherwise £10 per case mainland UK **EN PRIMEUR** Bordeaux, Burgundy, Port, Chateau Musar, South Africa. **C G M T**
✪ Star attractions *Starting at the beginning, Alsace and Beaujolais look spot-on. Bordeaux, Burgundy and Rhône are carefully chosen, and so I would trust their selections from other regions – sweeties and fortifieds are strong, too.*

Mayfair Cellars

Unit 3b, Farm Lane Trading Centre, 101 Farm Lane, London SW6 1QJ (020) 7386 7999 **FAX** (020) 7386

0202 E-MAIL sales@mayfaircellars. co.uk WEBSITE www.mayfaircellars. co.uk HOURS Mon–Fri 9–6 CARDS AmEx, MasterCard, Switch, Visa DELIVERY England & Wales free; Scotland ring for details MINIMUM ORDER 1 mixed case EN PRIMEUR Bordeaux, Burgundy. C M T
✪ **Star attractions** *Mail-order specialist in the classic regions of Europe – and some good wines from southern France –, from first-rate small producers not available in the high street. There are also wines from California and Tasmania and a full range of Jacquesson Champagnes.*

Millésima

87 Quai de Paludate, BP 89, F 33038 Bordeaux Cedex, France (0033) 5 57 80 88 13 FAX (0033) 5 57 80 88 19, Freephone 00800 26 73 32 89 or 0800 917 0352 E-MAIL adeprijck@millesima.com WEBSITE www.millesima.com HOURS Mon–Fri 8–5.30 CARDS AmEx, Diners, MasterCard, Switch, Visa DELIVERY Free for orders over £500, otherwise £20 EN PRIMEUR Bordeaux, Burgundy, Rhône. C M T
✪ **Star attractions** *Wines come direct from the châteaux of Bordeaux to Millésima's cellars, where 3 million bottles are stored. A sprinkling of established names from other French regions – and from other countries.*

Mills Whitcombe

New Lodge Farm, Peterchurch, Hereford HR3 6BJ (01981) 550028 FAX (01981) 550027 E-MAIL becky@millswhitcombe.co.uk WEBSITE www.millswhitcombe.co.uk HOURS Mon–Fri 10–6, out-of-hours answering machine for orders CARDS MasterCard, Solo, Switch, Visa DISCOUNTS 5% for wine collected from warehouse DELIVERY Free locally, £7.50 per consignment nationwide, free for orders over

£140 EN PRIMEUR Bordeaux, Burgundy. C G M T
✪ **Star attractions** *Young company with an expanding list of quality wines in a host of styles from a wide range of regions, especially Australia, Italy, Portugal, southern France and South Africa.*

Montrachet

MAIL ORDER 59 Kennington Road, London SE1 7PZ (020) 7928 1990 FAX (020) 7928 3415 E-MAIL charles@montrachetwine.com WEBSITE www.montrachetwine. com HOURS (Office and mail order) Mon–Fri 8.30–5.30 CARDS MasterCard, Switch, Visa DELIVERY England and Wales £12 including VAT, free for 3 or more cases; Scotland ring for details MINIMUM ORDER 1 unmixed case EN PRIMEUR Bordeaux, Burgundy. M T
✪ **Star attractions** *Impressive Burgundies, some very good Rhônes, and Bordeaux is excellent at all price levels. There's also a short but starry set of German wines.*

Moreno Wines

11 Marylands Road, London W9 2DU (020) 7286 0678 FAX (020) 7286 0513 E-MAIL merchant@ moreno-wines.co.uk WEBSITE www.morenowinedirect.co.uk HOURS Mon–Fri 4–9, Sat 12–10 CARDS AmEx, MasterCard, Switch, Visa DISCOUNTS 5% 1 or 2 cases, 10% 3 or more cases DELIVERY Free locally. M
✪ **Star attractions** *Fine and rare Spanish wines, but plenty of everyday drinking too, from upcoming regions like Aragon and Castilla y León. Then there's weird and wonderful stuff like Txomin from the Basque country, or Don P X Gran Reserva, a wonderful Christmas pudding of a wine from Montilla-Moriles in the sunny south at only £9.99. Also wines from South America.*

Moriarty Vintners

9 Wyndham Arcade, Cardiff CF10 1RH (02920) 229996 FAX (02920) 564814 E-MAIL sales@moriarty-vintners.com WEBSITE www.moriarty-vintners.com HOURS Mon–Sat 10–6 DISCOUNTS 5% off 6 bottles; 10% off 1 mixed case and regular special offers DELIVERY South Wales free, nationwide at cost MINIMUM ORDER 1 mixed case EN PRIMEUR Italy, Port, Rhône. C G M T
✪ Star attractions *This growing list concentrates on exciting gems from small producers. Italy is particularly strong and other regions with good coverage include the Languedoc, Bordeaux, Australia and Spain.*

Morris & Verdin

MAIL ORDER Unit 2, Bankside Industrial Estate, Sumner Street, London SE1 9J2 (020) 7921 5300 FAX (020) 7921 5333 E-MAIL sales@m-v.co.uk HOURS Mon–Fri 8–6 DISCOUNTS 10% unmixed cases DELIVERY Free central London; elsewhere £10 up to 3 cases, free 4 or more MINIMUM ORDER 1 mixed case. C G M T
✪ Star attractions *Burgundy specialist, with California coming on strong. Top producers are also cherry-picked from other areas: the rest of France, Germany, Austria, Spain, Portugal, Italy, Australia and New Zealand, and Tokaji from Hungary. From the US, besides no fewer than 12 producers from California, there's Domaine Drouhin from Oregon and Washington State's Andrew Will.*

Wm Morrison Supermarkets

HEAD OFFICE Hilmore House, Thorton Road, Bradford, W. Yorks BD8 9AX (01274) 494166 FAX (01274) 494831 CUSTOMER SERVICE (01274) 619703 130 licensed branches HOURS Variable, generally Mon–Sat 8–8, Sun 10–4 CARDS MasterCard, Switch, Visa. G T

✪ Star attractions *A good range of inexpensive, often tasty wines. Southern France, Chile and Argentina look particularly reliable.*

MR Wines

See Great Northern Wine

New Zealand Wines Direct

MAIL ORDER PO Box 476, London NW5 2NZ (020) 7482 0093 FAX (020) 7267 8400 E-MAIL sales@fwnz.co.uk or info@fwnz.co.uk WEBSITE www.fwnz.co.uk HOURS Mon–Sat 9–6 CARDS MasterCard, Visa DISCOUNTS 6 or more cases DELIVERY Free for 1 mixed case or more UK mainland MINIMUM ORDER 1 mixed case. M T
✪ Star attractions *Some of New Zealand's great wines: Bordeaux-style Larose from Stonyridge, plus wines from Ata Rangi, Hunter's, Kumeu River, Pegasus Bay, Palliser Estate, Quartz Reef, Redwood Valley and others.*

James Nicholson

27A Killyleagh Street, Crossgar, Co. Down, N Ireland BT30 9DQ (028) 4483 0091 FAX (028) 4483 0028 E-MAIL info@jnwine.com and shop@jnwine.com WEBSITE www.jnwine.com HOURS Mon–Sat 10–7 CARDS MasterCard, Switch, Visa DISCOUNTS 10% mixed case DELIVERY Free (1 case or more) in Eire and N Ireland; UK mainland £6.95 EN PRIMEUR Bordeaux, Burgundy, California. G M T
✪ Star attractions *Exceptionally appealing list: Bordeaux, Rhône and southern France are slightly ahead of the field, and there's a good selection of affordable Burgundy – as affordable as decent Burgundy ever is, anyway. Spain has new-wave wines from the likes of Artadi and Cellers de Capçanes, and there's excellent drinking from Germany. Everything is well chosen, mainly from small, committed growers around the world.*

Nickolls & Perks

37 High Street, Stourbridge, West Midlands DY8 1TA (01384) 394518 **FAX** (01384) 440786 **E-MAIL** sales@nickollsandperks.co.uk **WEBSITE** www.nickollsandperks.co.uk **HOURS** Mon–Fri 9.30–6, Sat 10–5 **CARDS** MasterCard, Visa **DISCOUNTS** negotiable **DELIVERY** £10 per consignment **MINIMUM ORDER** 1 mixed case. **EN PRIMEUR** Bordeaux. **C G M T**

✪ Star attractions *Wine shippers since 1797, Nickolls & Perks has always been important in the en primeur Bordeaux market. The wide-ranging list covers most areas and is particularly strong in France. Advice is available to clients wishing to develop their cellars or invest in wine. Search the terrific website for anniversary wines such as 1964 Cos d'Estournel, or a choice of 1955 ports.*

Nidderdale Fine Wines

2a High Street, Pateley Bridge, North Yorkshire HG3 5AW (01423) 711703 **E-MAIL** info@southaustralianwines.com **WEBSITE** www.southaustralianwines.com **HOURS** Tue–Fri 10–7, Sat 9–5.30, Sun 10–5.30 **CARDS** MasterCard, Switch, Visa **DISCOUNTS** 5% case discount on shop purchases **DELIVERY** £5 per case in England, Wales and southern Scotland; rest of UK £25 per case. Single bottle delivery negotiable. **G T**

✪ Star attractions *South Australia is the speciality here, with 400 wines broken down into regions, so if you want to see what's available from Barossa, Coonawarra, Adelaide Hills or Clare Valley, you need look no further. Also 350 or so wines from other parts of Australia and the rest of the world. look out for online offers and winemaker dinners.*

Noble Rot Wine Warehouses

18 Market Street, Bromsgrove, Worcestershire, B61 8DA

(01527) 575606 **FAX** (01527) 833133 **E-MAIL** info@noble-rot.co.uk **WEBSITE** www.noble-rot.co.uk **HOURS** Mon–Fri 10–7, Sat 9.30–6.30 **CARDS** MasterCard, Switch, Visa **DISCOUNTS** Various **DELIVERY** Free within 10 mile radius. **G T**

✪ Star attractions *What Noble Rot's customers want is good wine for current drinking, at £3 to £10 a bottle. Australia, Italy, France and Spain feature most strongly in a frequently changing list.*

The Nobody Inn

Doddiscombsleigh, Nr Exeter, Devon EX6 7PS (01647) 252394 **FAX** (01647) 252978 **E-MAIL** info@nobodyinn.co.uk **WEBSITE** www.nobodyinn.co.uk **HOURS** Mon–Sat 12–2.30 & 6–11 (summer); 6–11 (winter), Sun 12–3 & 7–10.30; or by appointment **CARDS** AmEx, MasterCard, Switch, Visa **DISCOUNTS** 5% per case **DELIVERY** £7.99 for 1 case, free over £150. **G M T**
• The Wine Company (01392) 477752 **FAX** (01392) 477759 **E-MAIL** sales@thewinecompany.biz **WEBSITE** www.thewinecompany.biz **HOURS** Mon–Fri 9.30–6, 24-hr ordering service **CARDS** AmEx, MasterCard, Switch, Visa **DELIVERY** Free for orders over £150.

✪ Star attractions *If you're going to eat here I advise you to turn up 2 hours early to browse through this extraordinary list. Australia rules, but there's something exciting from just about everywhere. Amazing range of sweet wines: Loire, of course, but also Greece's Samos Nectar Muscat and Vin de Constance from South Africa. The Wine Company is a new mail order venture for wines costing mainly between £5 and £10.*

Oddbins

HEAD OFFICE 31–33 Weir Road, London SW19 8UG (020) 8944 4400 **FAX** (020) 8944 4411

MAIL ORDER Oddbins Direct 0800 328 2323 **FAX** 0800 328 3848; 280 shops nationwide **WEBSITE** www.oddbins.com **HOURS** Generally Mon–Sat 10–10, Sun 10–8 in England & Wales, 12.30–8 Scotland **CARDS** AmEx, MasterCard, Switch, Visa **DISCOUNTS** regular offers on Champagne and sparkling wine, and general promotions **DELIVERY** (Stores) free locally for orders over £100; (online) £4.99 for 12 bottles or more, £6.99 for 1–11 bottles **EN PRIMEUR** Bordeaux. **G M T**

▸ **CALAIS STORE** Cité Europe, 139 Rue de Douvres, 62901, Coquelles Cedex, France (0033) 3 21 82 07 32 **FAX** (0033) 3 21 82 05 83 **PRE-ORDER** www.oddbins.com/ storefinder/calais.asp
✪ **Star attractions** New World pioneer or champion of the classics? Both, actually. Extensive Aussie selection, well-chosen Chileans and Argentinians; Spain, Italy, Greece, New Zealand, South Africa, Burgundy and Rhône all look good, and Languedoc is currently in the limelight. Great deals on Champagne. Now owned by French multinational group Castel, who are also owners of the Nicolas chain of wine shops and so let's hope the range remains as eclectic as ever.

OZ Wines

MAIL ORDER Freepost Lon 17656, London SW18 5BR, 0845 450 1261 **FAX** (020) 8870 8839 **E-MAIL** sales@ozwinesonline.co.uk **WEBSITE** www.ozwinesonline. co.uk **HOURS** Mon–Fri 9.30–7 **CARDS** Diners, MasterCard, Switch, Visa **DELIVERY** Free. **MINIMUM ORDER** 1 mixed case. **M**
✪ **Star attractions** Australian wines made by small wineries and real people, which means wines with the kind of thrilling flavours that Australians do better than anyone else. Small range from New Zealand.

Penistone Court Wine Cellars

The Railway Station, Penistone, Sheffield, South Yorkshire S36 6HP (01226) 766037 **FAX** (01226) 767310 **E-MAIL** pcwc@dircon.co.uk **HOURS** Tues–Fri 10–6, Sat 10–3 **CARDS** MasterCard, Switch, Visa **DELIVERY** Free locally, rest of UK mainland charged at cost 1 case or more **MINIMUM ORDER** 1 case. **G M**
✪ **Star attractions** A well-balanced list, with something from just about everywhere, mostly from familiar names. So, you've got Champagne (Pol Roger, Bollinger, Roederer and others), Burgundy, Beaujolais, Alsace, Loire, Rhône and a short list of clarets. Outside France, there's quite a good list from Italy, plus Austria, Spain, Chile, the USA, New Zealand and Australia (Brown Brothers, Stonier, Penfolds and De Bortoli).

Philglas & Swiggot

21 Northcote Road, Battersea,
London SW11 1NG (020) 7924 4494
• 64 Hill Rise, Richmond, London
TW10 6UB (020) 8332 6081 E-MAIL
info@philglas-swiggot.co.uk
WEBSITE www.philglas-
swiggot.co.uk
HOURS (Battersea) Mon–Sat 11–7,
Sun 12–5 (Richmond) Tue–Sat 11–7,
Sun 12–5 CARDS AmEx, MasterCard,
Switch, Visa DISCOUNTS 5% per case
DELIVERY Free 1 case locally. G M T
✪ Star attractions Excellent Aussie
selection – subtle, interesting
wines, not blockbuster brands. The
same philosophy applies to wines
they buy from elsewhere, so you'll
find serious Italians and good
French wines. Austria fits the bill
nicely and dessert wines are good
too.

Christopher Piper Wines

1 Silver Street, Ottery St Mary,
Devon EX11 1DB (01404) 814139
FAX (01404) 812100 E-MAIL
sales@christopherpiperwines.co.uk
WEBSITE
www.christopherpiperwines.co.uk
HOURS Mon–Fri 8.30–5.30, Sat
9–4.30 CARDS MasterCard, Switch,
Visa DISCOUNTS 5% mixed case, 10%
3 or more cases DELIVERY Free for
orders over £180, otherwise £5.25
per case MINIMUM ORDER 1 mixed
case EN PRIMEUR Bordeaux,
Burgundy, Rhône. C G M T
✪ Star attractions Oh, Oh, Oh what
a lovely list. There's nothing routine
here, just pages and pages of
interesting, well-chosen wines, with
lots of information to help you
make up your mind.

Terry Platt Wine Merchants

Council Street West, Llandudno
LL30 1ED (01492) 874099 FAX
(01492) 874788 E-MAIL info@
terryplattwines.co.uk WEBSITE
www.terryplattwines.co.uk
HOURS Mon–Fri 8.30–5.30 CARDS
AmEx, MasterCard, Switch, Visa

DELIVERY Free locally and UK
mainland 5 cases or more
MINIMUM ORDER 1 mixed case. G M T
✪ Star attractions A wide-ranging
list with a sprinkling of good
growers from most regions. New
World coverage has increased
recently: Argentina includes Terrazas
de los Andes and Humberto Canale;
from Chile there's Casa Lapostolle
and Montes; Australia has Cape
Mentelle and Nepenthe and South
Africa has Grangehurst.

Playford Ros

Middle Park House, Sowerby, Thirsk
Yorkshire YO7 3AH (01845) 526777
FAX (01845) 526888 E-MAIL
sales@playfordros.com
WEBSITE www.playfordros.com
HOURS Mon–Fri 8–5 CARDS
MasterCard, Visa DISCOUNTS 2.5%
on orders over 6 cases DELIVERY
Free Yorkshire, Derbyshire, Durham,
Newcastle; elsewhere on UK
mainland (per case), £10 1 case,
£6.50 2 cases, £5 3 cases, £4 4 cases
free 5 cases MINIMUM ORDER 1
mixed case EN PRIMEUR Bordeaux,
Burgundy. C G M T
✪ Star attractions A carefully
chosen list, with reassuringly
recognizable representatives from
Bordeaux and Burgundy, Alsace, the
Rhône and the Loire. Similar
standards apply elsewhere, with
Australia looking exceptional, and
there is a good selection of wines at
around the £5 to £6 mark.

Portland Wine Co

16 North Parade, off Norris Road,
Sale, Cheshire M33 3JS (0161) 962
8752 FAX (0161) 905 1291 • 152a
Ashley Road, Hale WA15 9SA (0161)
928 0357 • 82 Chester Road,
Macclesfield SK11 8DL (01625)
616147 E-MAIL enquiries@
portlandwine.co.uk WEBSITE
www.portlandwine.co.uk
HOURS Mon–Sat 10–10, Sun 12–9.30
CARDS MasterCard, Switch, Visa
DISCOUNTS 5% 2 cases or more, 10%

5 cases or more DELIVERY Free locally 1 case or more, £10 + VAT per consignment nationwide EN PRIMEUR Bordeaux. C T

✪ Star attractions *Spain, Portugal and Burgundy are the specialities here and there is also a promising-looking list of lesser clarets, as well as more expensive, stunning older vintages. This consumer-friendly list has something at every price level from around the world.*

Raeburn Fine Wines

21–23 Comely Bank Road, Edinburgh EH4 1DS (0131) 343 1159 FAX (0131) 332 5166 E-MAIL sales@raeburnfinewines.com WEBSITE www.raeburnfine wines.com HOURS Mon–Sat 9.30–6, Sun 12.30–5 CARDS AmEx, MasterCard, Switch, Visa DISCOUNTS 5% unsplit case, 2.5% mixed DELIVERY Free local area 1 or more cases (usually); elsewhere at cost EN PRIMEUR Australia, Bordeaux, Burgundy, California, Germany, Italy, Languedoc-Roussillon, Loire, New Zealand, Rhône. G M T

✪ Star attractions *Everything here is carefully chosen, usually from small growers: if you want obvious choices you won't like this list, but if you want to try interesting wines from an impressive array of vintages you'll be more than happy. Burgundy is something of a speciality and in the Loire there are oodles of Vouvrays from Huet, in vintages going back to 1924. Italy, Germany, Austria, New Zealand, Australia and California all look fabulous. Ports from Niepoort.*

Reid Wines

The Mill, Marsh Lane, Hallatrow, Nr Bristol BS39 6EB (01761) 452645 FAX (01761) 453642 HOURS Mon–Fri 9–5.30 CARDS MasterCard, Visa (3% charge) DELIVERY Free within 25 miles of Hallatrow (Bristol), and in central London for orders over 2 cases C G M T

✪ Star attractions *Reid's is one of the lists I look forward to reading most: it's full of pithy comments alongside its fabulous array of older vintages. Five clarets from 1975 were 'heralded at birth, scorned in middle age, graceful and delicious (some of them) now.' A mix of great old wines, some old duds and splendid current stuff. Italy, USA, Australia, port and Madeira look tremendous.*

La Réserve

56 Walton Street, Knightsbridge, London SW3 1RB (020) 7589 2020 FAX (020) 7581 0250 • 7 Grant Road, London SW11 2NU (020) 7978 5601 • 29 Heath Street, Hampstead, London NW3 6TR (020) 7435 6845 • Milroys of Soho, 3 Greek Street, London W1V 6NX (020) 7437 2385 • 203 Munster Road, London SW6 6BX (020) 7381 6930 E-MAIL realwine@la-reserve.co.uk WEBSITE www.la-reserve.co.uk HOURS Vary from shop to shop CARDS AmEx, MasterCard, Switch, Visa DISCOUNTS 5% per case except accounts DELIVERY Free 1 case or more central London and orders over £200 on UK mainland. Otherwise £7.50 EN PRIMEUR Bordeaux, Burgundy, Italy, Rhône, Port. C G M T

✪ Star attractions *Varied, intelligent list. Burgundy, Bordeaux, the Loire, Alsace, Spain, Italy, North America, Australia, New Zealand and South Africa are all excellent, with well-chosen wines (Jermann, Gaja, Vajra and Argiano in Italy, for example).*

Richardson & Sons

2A Marlborough Street, Whitehaven, Cumbria CA28 7LL FAX/TEL (01946) 65334 E-MAIL mailwines@aol.com HOURS Mon–Sat 10–5.30 CARDS AmEx, Delta, MasterCard, Switch, Visa DELIVERY Free locally; UK mainland £10 first case and £2 each additional case; orders over £150 free. G M T

✪ **Star attractions** *It's the only place in Cumbria stocking Ch. Latour and Opus One, but in general Richardson & Sons carefully select from interesting small producers, preferring 'little hidden gems' to big-name brands. Rioja is chosen to represent various styles. Very good stuff from South Africa.*

Howard Ripley

25 Dingwall Road, London SW18 3AZ (020) 8877 3065 **FAX** (020) 8877 0029 **E-MAIL** info@howardripley.com **WEBSITE** www.howardripley.com **HOURS** Mon–Fri 9–8, Sat 9–1 **CARDS** MasterCard, Switch, Visa **DELIVERY** Minimum charge £9.50 + VAT, free UK mainland on orders over £500 ex-VAT **MINIMUM ORDER** 1 mixed case **EN PRIMEUR** Burgundy, Germany. **C M T**

✪ **Star attractions** *If you're serious about Burgundy, this is one of perhaps half a dozen lists that you need. Yes, the wines are expensive – great Burgundy is expensive – but they're not excessive. The German range is also excellent.*

Roberson

348 Kensington High Street, London W14 8NS (020) 7371 2121 **FAX** (020) 7371 4010 **E-MAIL** retail@roberson.co.uk **WEBSITE** www.robersonwinemerchant.co.uk **HOURS** Mon–Sat 10–8 **CARDS** AmEx, Diners, MasterCard, Switch, Visa **DISCOUNTS MAIL ORDER** 5% on unmixed cases; shop 10% unmixed or mixed cases **DELIVERY** Free delivery within London, otherwise £15 per case **EN PRIMEUR** Bordeaux, Burgundy, Port. **C G M T**

✪ **Star attractions** *Fine and rare wines, sold by the bottle. Clarets back to 1900, with plenty from the great 1989 and 1990 vintages. If you fancy a bottle of 1945 Ch. Mouton-Rothschild at £5,500, you'll find it here. Excellent for Italy and port.*

The RSJ Wine Company

33 Coin Street, London SE1 9NR (020) 7928 4554 **FAX** (020) 7928 9768 **E-MAIL** tom.king@rsj.uk.com **WEBSITE** www.rsj.uk.com **HOURS** Mon–Fri 9–6, answering machine at other times **CARDS** MasterCard, Visa **DELIVERY** Free central London, minimum 1 case; England and Wales (per case), £14.10 1 case, £10.25 2 cases or more. **G M T**

✪ **Star attractions** *A roll-call of great Loire names. From Savennières there is Domaine aux Moines, from Chinon J & C Baudry, from Saumur Domaine des Roches Neuves, to mention just a few. And now there are wines from outside the Loire as well: Beaujolais, Alsace, Italy, Australia, New Zealand.*

Safeway

Now owned by Wm Morrison plc (see page 127)

Sainsbury's

HEAD OFFICE 33 Holborn, London EC1N 2HT (020) 7695 6000 **CUSTOMER SERVICE** 0800 636262; 524 stores (including Savacentres) **WEBSITE** www. sainsburys.co.uk **HOURS** Variable, some 24 hrs, locals generally Mon–Sat 7–11, Sun 10 or 11–4 **CARDS** AmEx, MasterCard, Switch, Visa **DISCOUNTS** 5% for 6 bottles or more **G M T** • **MAIL ORDER** 0800 917 4092 **FAX** 0800 917 4095 • **CALAIS STORE** La Boutique Sainsbury's, Centre Commercial Auchan, Route de Boulogne, 62100 Calais, France (0033) 3 21 82 38 48 **FAX** (0033) 3 21 36 01 91 **PREORDER** www.sainsburys.co.uk/calais

✪ **Star attractions** *Sainsbury's manages to cater for bargain hunters as well as appealing to lovers of good-value wine higher up the scale. There's a short list of affordable clarets, improving Italians, and a willingness to venture into areas like Morocco. Chile and Argentina are good too.*

Savage Selection

The Ox House, Market Place, Northleach, Cheltenham, Glos GL54 3EG (01451) 860896 FAX (01451) 860996 • The Ox House Shop and Wine Bar at same address (01451) 860680 E-MAIL wine@savage selection.co.uk WEBSITE www.savageselection.co.uk HOURS Office: Mon–Fri 9–6; shop: Tue/Wed 10–7.30, Thur–Fri 10–10, Sat 10–3 CARDS AmEx, MasterCard, Switch, Visa DELIVERY Free locally 1 case, elsewhere on UK mainland free 3 cases, otherwise £10 per consignment EN PRIMEUR Bordeaux. C G M T

✪ Star attractions One of the delights of this list is that Mark Savage takes the trouble to find wines for himself, and he really does go after the maverick personalities. A classic example is the Big Men in Tights rosé (£8) from Bloodwood, made in Australia by Stephen Doyle. There's also a weird but inspired Kékfrankos/Kekoporto from Hungary (£5.88) tasting of white pepper and sweet tomato flesh, and a Chardonnay from Idaho (see page 29). France is also strong, with wines from Bordeaux, Burgundy and Provence.

Seckford Wines

Dock Lane, Melton, Suffolk IP12 1PE (01394) 446622 FAX (01394) 446633 E-MAIL sales@seckfordwines.co.uk WEBSITE www.seckfordwines.co.uk CARDS MasterCard, Switch, Visa DELIVERY £10 per consignment, UK mainland; elsewhere at cost. MINIMUM ORDER 1 mixed case. C

✪ Star attractions Bordeaux, Burgundy and the Rhône are the stars of this list, and if you prefer older vintages, Seckford have got plenty of these. There's serious stuff from Italy, Spain and Austria, too.

Somerfield

HEAD OFFICE Somerfield House, Whitchurch Lane, Bristol BS14 0TJ (0117) 935 9359 FAX (0117) 935 6669; 670 Somerfield stores and 567 Kwiksave stores nationwide WEBSITE www.somerfield.co.uk HOURS Mon–Sat 8–8, Sun 10–4 CARDS MasterCard, Switch, Visa DISCOUNTS 5% off 6 bottles DELIVERY Free local delivery for orders over £25 in selected stores M T

✪ Star attractions The focus is on wines under £5, and these tend to come from the Languedoc, South America, Spain and Portugal. Sparkling wines are generally good, from vintage Cava to the own-label Prince William Champagne.

Sommelier Wine Co

23 St George's Esplanade, St Peter Port, Guernsey, Channel Islands, GY1 2BG (01481) 721677 FAX (01481) 716818 HOURS Mon–Thur 10–5.30, Fri 10–6, Sat 9.30–5.30 CARDS MasterCard, Switch, Visa DISCOUNTS 5% 1 case or more DELIVERY Free locally 1 unmixed case. Customs legislation restricts the shipping of wine to the UK mainland. G T

✪ Star attractions An excellent list, with interesting, unusual wines. It's a big selection, too: there are yards of lovely subtle Italian whites and well-made reds, and lots of Loires and Beaujolais. Burgundy, South Africa, Chile and Argentina all look good, though Australia outdoes them all.

Frank Stainton Wines

3 Berry's Yard, Finkle Street, Kendal, Cumbria LA9 4AB (01539) 731886 FAX (01539) 730396 E-MAIL admin@stainton-wines.co.uk HOURS Mon–Sat 9–5.30 CARDS MasterCard, Switch, Visa DISCOUNTS 5% mixed case DELIVERY Free Cumbria and North Lancashire; elsewhere (per case) £9 1 case, £6 2–4 cases, £4 5–9 cases, 10 cases free. G M T

✪ Star attractions Some interesting Burgundy growers, but on the whole Bordeaux is better. Italy has a

selection of leading names. Chile
includes the wines of Casa Silva,
which have real character and
subtlety. Also Three Choirs wines
from England.

Stevens Garnier

47 West Way, Botley, Oxford OX2
0JF (01865) 263303 **FAX** (01865)
791594 **E-MAIL** shop@stevens
garnier.co.uk **HOURS** Mon–Wed
10–6, Thur–Fri 10–7, Sat 9.30–6
CARDS AmEx, MasterCard, Switch,
Visa, Solo **DISCOUNTS** 5% on an
unmixed case **DELIVERY** Free locally;
'competitive rates' elsewhere. **G T**
✿ **Star attractions** 'Regional
France' is a strength here, meaning
there's at least one representative
from most regions: this is one of
the few places in the UK you can
buy wine from Savoie. Portugal is
from quality-conscious Sogrape.
The New World has some pleasant
surprises: Grant Burge and Willow
Bridge from Australia, Carmen
from Chile, Chateau des Charmes
from Canada.

Stone, Vine & Sun

No. 13 Humphrey Farms, Hazeley
Road, Twyford, Winchester SO21 1QA
0845 061 4604 **FAX** (01962) 717545
E-MAIL sales@stonevine.co.uk
WEBSITE www.stonevine.co.uk
HOURS Mon–Fri 9–6, Sat 9.30–1
CARDS MasterCard, Switch, Visa
DISCOUNTS 5% on an unmixed case
DELIVERY £3.50 per case. Prices vary
for Scottish highlands and islands
and N Ireland **MINIMUM ORDER** 1
mixed case. **G M T**
✿ **Star attractions** Lovely list
marked by enthusiasm and passion
for the subject. Lots of interesting
stuff, especially from France, but
also from Germany, Austria and
elsewhere – and they're determined
to do it properly: whenever I'm
nosing about the byways and
backroads of France, who do I meet
but someone from Stone, Vine &
Sun doing the same thing?

Sunday Times Wine Club

New Aquitaine House, Exeter
Way, Theale, Reading, Berks
RG7 4PL **ORDER LINE** 0870 220 0010
FAX 0870 220 0030 **E-MAIL**
orders@sundaytimeswineclub.co.uk
WEBSITE www.sundaytimeswine
club.co.uk **HOURS** 24-hr answering
machine **CARDS** AmEx, Diners,
MasterCard, Switch, Visa
DELIVERY £4.99 per order
EN PRIMEUR Australia, Bordeaux,
Burgundy, Rhône. **C M T**
✿ **Star attractions** Essentially the
same list as Laithwaites (see page
122), though the special offers
come round at different times. The
membership fee is £10 per annum.
The club runs tours and tasting
events for its members.

T & W Wines

5 Station Way, Brandon, Suffolk IP27
0BH (01842) 814414 **FAX** (01842)
819967

E-MAIL contact@tw-wines.com
WEBSITE www.tw-wines.com **HOURS**
Mon–Fri. 9.30–5.30, occasional Sat
9.30–1 **CARDS** AmEx, Diners,
MasterCard, Visa **DELIVERY** (most
areas) 7–23 bottles £10.95 + VAT, 2
or more cases free **EN PRIMEUR**
Burgundy. **C G M T**
✪ **Star attractions** *The list is a good
one, particularly if you're looking
for Burgundy, Rhône, Alsace or the
Loire, but prices are not especially
low, and when working out the
final cost remember that they
exclude VAT. There's an amazing list
of over 240 half bottles, including
the superb sweet wines of Willi
Opitz, from Austria, and 25
biodynamic wines from France.*

Tanners

26 Wyle Cop, Shrewsbury,
Shropshire SY1 1XD (01743) 234500
FAX (01743) 234501 • 4 St Peter's
Square, Hereford HR1 2PG (01432)
272044 **FAX** (01432) 263316 • 36
High Street, Bridgnorth WV16 4DB
(01746) 763148 **FAX** (01746) 769798•
Severn Farm Enterprise Park,
Welshpool SY21 7DF (01938) 552542
FAX (01938) 556565 **E-MAIL**
sales@tanners-wines.co.uk **WEBSITE**
www.tanners-wines.co.uk **HOURS**
Shrewsbury Mon–Sat 9–6,
branches 9–5.30 **CARDS** AmEx,
MasterCard, Switch, Visa **DISCOUNTS**
5% 1 mixed case (cash & collection);
2.5% for 3 mixed cases, 5% for 5,
7.5% for 10 (**MAIL ORDER**) **DELIVERY**
Free 1 mixed case or more locally, or
nationally over £80, otherwise
£7.50 **EN PRIMEUR** Bordeaux,
Burgundy, Rhône, Port. **G M T**
✪ **Star attractions** *The sort of list
from which it's extremely difficult
to choose, because you simply want
everything on it. There are lots of
lovely Rhônes; Bordeaux and
Burgundy are both terrific;
Germany is outstanding, and there
are even a couple of wines from
Switzerland and Lebanon. Spain
and Italy look very good, and*
*Australia, South Africa and
California all show what these
places can do.*

Tesco

HEAD OFFICE Tesco House, PO Box 18,
Delamare Road, Cheshunt EN8 9SL
(01992) 632222 **FAX** (01992)
630794, **CUSTOMER SERVICE** 0800
505555; 916 licensed branches **E-MAIL** customer.services@tesco.co.uk
WEBSITE www.tesco.co.uk
HOURS Variable **CARDS** MasterCard,
Switch, Visa **DISCOUNT** 5% on 6
bottles or more **G M T**
• **CALAIS STORE** Tesco Vin Plus, Cité
Europe, 122 Boulevard du Kent,
62231 Coquelles, France (0033) 3 21
46 02 70 **WEBSITE** www.tesco.com/
vinplus; www.tesco-france.com
HOURS Mon–Sat 8.30–10pm
✪ **Star attractions** *This is looking
increasingly like a place to do some
serious wine shopping – the Tesco
Finest range can reveal some true
beauties, well worth the extra quid
or two they'll cost. And there are
still lots of cheapies for when your
budget is more of the baked beans
on toast sort.*

Thresher Group: Thresher Wine Shops and Wine Rack

HEAD OFFICE Enjoyment Hall,
Bessemer Road, Welwyn Garden
City, Herts AL7 1BL (01707) 387200
FAX (01707) 387350 **WEBSITE**
www.threshergroup.com; 1,250
Thresher Wine Shops, 200 Wine
Rack stores **HOURS** Mon–Sat 10–10
(some 10.30), Sun 11–10, Scotland
12.30–10.30 **CARDS** MasterCard,
Switch, Visa **DELIVERY** Free locally,
some branches. **G T**
✪ **Star attractions** *A major high
street presence, Thresher wine
shops are presumably a faithful
reflection of everyday wine
drinking in Britain. Threshers have a
large number of stores and have
undergone some justified criticism
recently about cutting down their
range of wines. But there's nothing*

inherently wrong with a reduced range – now down to 400–500 wines – so long as you take greater care in sourcing the wines you do decide to stock, which they seem determined to do.

Turville Valley Wines

The Firs, Potter Row, Great Missenden, Bucks HP16 9LT (01494) 868818 **FAX** (01494) 868832 **E-MAIL** info@turville-valley-wines.com **WEBSITE** www.turville-valley-wines.com **HOURS** Mon–Fri 9–5.30 **CARDS** None **DELIVERY** By arrangement **MINIMUM ORDER** £300/12 bottles. **C M**

✪ **Star attractions** *Serious wines for serious spenders. The Bordeaux is all classic, mostly mature stuff – no lesser wines here – and there are buckets of Domaine de la Romanée-Conti Burgundies. There are top names too from Spain, Italy, the Rhône, California (Dominus, Harlan Estate, Dalla Valle, Opus One) and odds and ends from all over.*

Unwins

HEAD OFFICE Birchwood House, Victoria Road, Dartford, Kent DA1 5AJ (01322) 272711 **FAX** (01322) 294469; 400 branches in southern and eastern England **E-MAIL** info@unwins.co.uk **WEBSITE** www.unwins.co.uk **HOURS** Variable, usually Mon–Sat 10–10, Sun 11–10 **CARDS** AmEx, Diners, MasterCard, Switch, Visa **DISCOUNTS** 10% on mixed case, 5% on 6 bottles and regular special offers **DELIVERY** Free locally **G T**

✪ **Star attractions** *Unwins is a very important retailer in the South-East, but has been lacking direction recently. This year there seems to be a new mood about the company, and the beginnings of a more exciting range in the shops. The New World selection in particular is starting to balance big brands with more interesting examples.*

Valvona & Crolla

19 Elm Row, Edinburgh EH7 4AA (0131) 556 6066 **FAX** (0131) 556 1668 **E-MAIL** wine@valvonacrolla.co.uk **WEBSITE** www.valvonacrolla.com **HOURS** Mon–Sat 8–6.30, Sun 11–5 **CARDS** AmEx, MasterCard, Switch, Visa **DISCOUNTS** 7% 1–3 cases, 10% 4 or more **DELIVERY** Free on orders over £125, £6 otherwise for 8 day service, £8 for next day service. **G M T**

✪ **Star attractions** *If you're fond of Italian wines you should be shopping here. The list has dozens and dozens of wines from Piedmont and Tuscany, and there are others from Lombardy, Basilicata, Calabria, the Marche, Sicily, Sardinia, the Veneto, and terrific dessert wines. It's a simply fabulous selection, and at all prices. There are wines from Australia, New Zealand, France, Argentina, Spain and Portugal and elsewhere, but they are not what V&C is really about.*

Villeneuve Wines

1 Venlaw Court, Peebles, Scotland EH45 8AE (01721) 722500 **FAX** (01721) 729922 • 82 High Street, Haddington EH41 3ET (01620) 822224 • 49A Broughton Street, Edinburgh EH1 3RJ (0131) 558 8441 **E-MAIL** wines@villeneuvewines.com **WEBSITE** www.villeneuvewines.com **HOURS** (Peebles) Mon–Sat 9–8, Sun 12.30–5.30; (Haddington) Mon–Thur 10–7, Fri 10–8, Sat 9–8; (Edinburgh) Mon–Sat 9–10, Sun 12.30–10 **CARDS** AmEx, MasterCard, Switch, Visa **DISCOUNTS** 5% per case **DELIVERY** 48-hour service. Free locally, £7.50 per case elsewhere. **G M T**

✪ **Star attractions** *Italy, California, Australia and New Zealand are all marvellous here. Italy has Pieropan, Planeta, Aldo Conterno, Aldo Vajra, Isole e Olena, Jermann, Allegrini and many others. From California there are wines from Duckhorn, Shafer,*

Stag's Leap, Ridge and Joseph Phelps. Australia includes Brokenwood, Mount Langi Ghiran and Plantagenet, New Zealand has Mount Difficulty, Cloudy Bay and Felton Road. Spain is clearly an enthusiasm, and Chile, Argentina and South Africa are well chosen.

Vinceremos

74 Kirkgate, Leeds LS2 7DJ (0113) 244 0002 FAX (0113) 288 4566 E-MAIL info@vinceremos.co.uk WEBSITE www.vinceremos.co.uk HOURS Mon–Sat 8.30–5.30 CARDS AmEx, Delta, MasterCard, Switch, Visa, DISCOUNTS 5% on 5 cases or over, 10% on 10 cases or over DELIVERY £5.95 per order, free 5 cases or more MINIMUM ORDER 1 mixed case M
✪ Star attractions *Organic specialist, with a wide-ranging list of wines that I'd actually like to drink: Guy Bossard's Muscadet, Huet's Vouvray, Sedlescombe Vineyard in England, Millton Vineyard in New Zealand, Fetzer's Bonterra wines from California and a whole page of reds and whites from Morocco.*

Vin du Van

MAIL ORDER Colthups, The Street, Appledore, Kent TN26 2BX (01233) 758727 FAX (01233) 758389 HOURS Mon–Fri 9–5 CARDS Delta, MasterCard, Switch, Visa DELIVERY Free locally; elsewhere £5.95 for first case, further cases free. Highlands & islands ask for quote MINIMUM ORDER 1 case. G M
✪ Star attractions *Quirky, star-studded Australian list, the kind of inspired lunacy I'd take to read on the first manned space trip to Mars.*

Vintage Roots

Farley Farms, Reading Road, Arborfield, Berkshire, RG2 9HT (0118) 976 1999 FAX (0118) 976 1998 HOURS Mon–Fri 8.30–5.30, Saturdays in December E-MAIL info@vintageroots.co.uk WEBSITE www.vintageroots.co.uk CARDS Delta, MasterCard, Switch, Visa DISCOUNTS 5% on 5 cases or over DELIVERY £5.95 for single case, £6.95 2–5 cases, free 6 cases or more. T
✪ Star attractions *Everything on this list is organic, beginning with a choice of Champagnes and other fizz and ending with beers and cider. Chile looks good – as indeed it should – alongside France (Côtes de Bourg from Ch. Falfas in Bordeaux, for example), Spain and Italy.*

Virgin Wines

MAIL ORDER The Loft, St James' Mill, Whitefriars, Norwich NR3 1TN (01603) 686688 FAX (01603) 619277 CUSTOMER SERVICE 0870 164 9593 E-MAIL help@virginwines.co.uk WEBSITE www.virginwines.com HOURS (office) Mon–Fri 8–7, Sat–Sun 10–5, Internet 24 hrs CARDS AmEx, MasterCard, Switch, Visa DELIVERY £4.99 for UK, N Ireland and Scottish Highlands, £6.99 for Saturday delivery within M25 MINIMUM ORDER 1 case. G M
✪ Star attractions *Internet retailer with hundreds of reasonably priced wines from all around the world. The list is organized by style rather than by grape variety, region or vintage and encourages the buyer to branch out and try new wines.*

Waitrose

HEAD OFFICE Doncastle Road, Southern Industrial Area, Bracknell, Berks RG12 8YA, CUSTOMER SERVICE 0800 188884; 143 licensed stores E-MAIL customerservice@waitrose.co.uk WEBSITE www.waitrose.com HOURS Mon–Tue 8.30–7 or 8, Wed–Thur 8.30–8, Fri 8.30–9, Sat 8.30–7, Sun 10–4 or 11–5 CARDS AmEx, Delta, MasterCard, Switch, Visa DISCOUNTS 5% for 6 bottles or more DELIVERY Home Delivery and Waitrosedeliver

Thank you... Thank you."

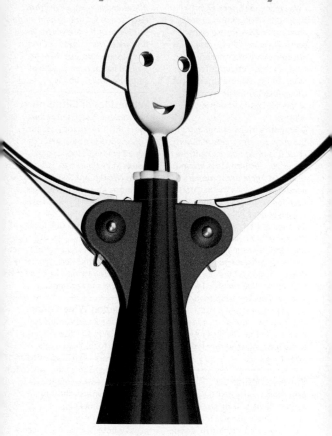

available at selected branches
EN PRIMEUR Bordeaux, Port. G T
• WAITROSE WINE DIRECT 24-hr
freephone 0800 188881 or order
online at www.waitrose.com
E-MAIL winedirect@waitrose.co.uk
DISCOUNTS Vary monthly on
featured cases DELIVERY Free for
orders of £75 or more throughout
UK mainland and Isle of Wight,
otherwise £4.95 per delivery
address.
✪ Star attractions *Still ahead of
the other supermarkets in quality,
value and imagination. Waitrose
brings you the best from around
the world. There are some very
good clarets – such as the Côtes de
Castillon Seigneurs d'Aiguilhe at
£7.99 (see page 52) – and
Burgundies, and some wonderful
discoveries from southern France,
the Rhône and the Loire. Italy,
Germany, Portugal and Spain all
deliver the goods, and Australia
and New Zealand have wines to
suit every pocket. Despite its
reputation for being a tad
expensive, we found lots of really
tasty stuff at under £5. All Waitrose
wines are available from Waitrose
Wine Direct.*

Waterloo Wine Co
OFFICE AND WAREHOUSE 6 Vine Yard,
London SE1 1QL SHOP 59–61 Lant
Street, London SE1 1QL (020) 7403
7967 FAX (020) 7357 6976 E-MAIL
sales@waterloowine.co.uk
WEBSITE www.waterloowine.co.uk
HOURS Mon–Fri 10–6.30, Sat 10–5
CARDS AmEx, MasterCard, Switch,
Visa DELIVERY Free 5 cases in
central London (otherwise £5);
elsewhere, 1 case £10, 2 cases £7.50
each. G T
✪ Star attractions *A very quirky,
personal list, strong in the Loire
and making something of a
speciality of the wines of the
Waipara region of Canterbury, New
Zealand (Waipara West, Waipara
Springs and Mark Rattray).*

*Waterloo are the UK agents for
Minervois from Domaine La Tour
Boisée and also list wines from
Hewitson in South Australia – and
this is one of the few places you'll
find wines from Slovenia, Croatia
and Montenegro. But there are
finds in lots of regions, such as
Sauternes and Germany.*

Whitesides of Clitheroe
Shawbridge Street, Clitheroe,
Lancs BB7 1NA (01200) 422281
FAX (01200) 427129 E-MAIL
wine@whitesideswine.co.uk
HOURS Mon–Fri 9–5.30, Sat 9–5
CARDS MasterCard, Switch, Visa
DISCOUNTS 5% per case DELIVERY
Free locally, elsewhere at cost.
G M T
✪ Star attractions *A safe list of
familiar names and flavours. I can
find a reasonable number of wines
I'd choose to drink here, especially
from the New World, but also from
Spain, Italy and Portugal.*

Wimbledon Wine Cellar
1 Gladstone Road, Wimbledon,
London SW19 1QU (020) 8540
9979 FAX (020) 8540 9399
• 84 Chiswick High Road, London
W4 1SY (020) 8994 7989 FAX (020)
8994 3683 E-MAIL enquiries@
wimbledonwinecellar.com or
chiswick@wimbledon
winecellar.com WEBSITE
www.wimbledonwine cellar.com
HOURS (Wimbledon) Mon–Sat 10–9
(Chiswick) Mon–Sat 10–9, Sun 11–7
CARDS AmEx, MasterCard, Switch,
Visa DISCOUNTS 10% off 1 case
(with a few exceptions) DELIVERY
Free within the M25. Courier
charges elsewhere. EN PRIMEUR
Burgundy, Bordeaux, Tuscany.
C G M T
✪ Star attractions *Top names from
Italy, Burgundy, Bordeaux, Rhône,
Loire – and some of the best of the
New World, especially Australia and
California. They don't issue a list, as
stock changes so frequently, so*

you'll just have to go along to one of the shops and dig out your own treasure or look at their website.

Wine & Beer World (Majestic)

HEAD OFFICE Majestic House, Otterspool Way, Watford, Herts WD25 8WW (01923) 298200 FAX (01923) 819105 PRE-ORDER (01923) 298297 • Rue du Judée, Zone Marcel Doret, Calais 62100, France (0033) 3 21 97 63 00 • Centre Commercial Carrefour, Quai L'Entrepôt, Cherbourg 50100, France (0033) 2 33 22 23 22 • Unit 3A, Zone La Française, Coquelles 62331, France (0033) 3 21 82 93 64 E-MAIL info@wineandbeer.co.uk WEBSITE www.wineandbeer.co.uk HOURS (Calais) 7 days 7–10 (Cherbourg) Mon–Sat 8.30–8 (Coquelles) 7 days 9–8. All stores open bank holidays at the usual times CARDS MasterCard, Switch, Visa. T

✪ Star attractions The French arm of Majestic, with three branches all handy for trips across the Channel. Calais is the largest branch, Coquelles the nearest to the Channel Tunnel terminal, while Cherbourg has a more limited range of wines. English-speaking staff. Savings of up to 50% on UK prices.

Winemark

3 Duncrue Place, Belfast BT3 9BU, 028 9074 6274 FAX 028 9075 1755; 71 branches E-MAIL info@winemark.com WEBSITE www.winemark.com HOURS Branches vary, but in general Mon–Sat 10–10, Sun 12–8 CARDS Delta, MasterCard, Switch, Visa DISCOUNTS 5% on 6–11 bottles, 10% on 12 bottles or more. G M T ✪ Star attractions Winemark is strong in the New World: there is lots to choose from in Australia (Peter Lehmann, Chateau Reynella

and Hardys right up to Eileen Shiraz at £49.99), New Zealand (Esk Valley and Villa Maria), California (Geyser Peak and Byron, among others), Chile (Errázuriz Wild Ferment Chardonnay and Carmen Nativa Cabernet Sauvignon), and there's a good list of Bordeaux from older vintages.

wine-pages-shop.com

✪ Now, this sounds like a great idea, it's a website set up by wine writer Tom Cannavan, and offers mixed cases selected by Tom (with tasting notes to help you choose) and supplied direct from UK retailers. Tom has negotiated some exclusive discounts and persuaded the retailers to waive their delivery charges, so there are some truly amazing savings to be made.

Wine Rack
See Thresher Group.

WATERLOO WINE CO

61 Lant Street
London
SE1 1QL

Tel: 020 7403 7967

Email: sales@waterloowine.co.uk
www.waterloowine.co.uk

Agents for
independent producers
from around the world,
including
Waipara West.

www.waiparawest.com

The Wine Society

Gunnels Wood Road, Stevenage, Herts SG1 2BG (01438) 741177 FAX (01438) 761167 ORDER LINE (01438) 740222 E-MAIL memberservices@ thewinesociety.com WEBSITE www.thewinesociety.com HOURS Mon–Fri 8.30–9, Sat 9–2; showroom: Mon–Thurs 10–6, Fri 10–7, Sat 9.30–5.30 CARDS MasterCard, Switch, Visa DISCOUNTS (per case) £1 for 5–9, £2 for 10 or more, £3 for collection DELIVERY Free 1 case or more UK mainland and N Ireland. Collection facility at Hesdin, France, at French rates of duty and VAT EN PRIMEUR Bordeaux, Burgundy, Germany, Port, Rhône. C G M T

✪ Star attractions *The Wine Society has an inspired wine-buying team and this is an outstanding list. Bordeaux is excellent, with masses of well-chosen affordable wines as well as big names; Burgundy ditto; Rhône ditto; Loire, Italy, Spain, Portugal, all ditto, and lovely, classy New World wines. If you close your eyes and choose wines from this list with a pin, you'll always get something wonderful. The own label wines are as good as ever. You have to be a member to buy wine, but it costs only £40 for life and although it is necessary to be proposed by an existing member to join, the secretary of the society will propose you if you don't happen to know any members.*

Wine Treasury

MAIL ORDER 69–71 Bondway, London SW8 1SQ (020) 7793 9999 FAX (020) 7793 8080 E-MAIL quality@winetreasury.com WEBSITE www.winetreasury.com HOURS Mon–Fri 9.30–6.30 CARDS MasterCard, Switch, Visa DISCOUNTS 10% for unmixed dozens DELIVERY £10 per case, free 2 or more cases over £100, England and Wales; Scotland phone for more details MINIMUM ORDER 1 mixed case. M T

✪ Star attractions *California is a speciality here. There are the stunning Cabernet Sauvignons and Chardonnays from Stag's Leap Wine Cellars, Zinfandel from Cline Cellars, lots of tasty stuff from Joseph Phelps and much, much more. Italy looks just as good, with stars such as Sandrone and Roberto Voerzio from Piedmont, Tuscany's Castello di Ama and Sicily's Cusumano. But these top names don't come cheap.*

The Winery

4 Clifton Road, London W9 1SS (020) 7286 6475 FAX (020) 7286 2733 E-MAIL info@thewinery.co.uk HOURS Mon–Sat 11–9.30, Sun and public holidays 12–8 CARDS MasterCard, Switch, Visa DISCOUNTS 5% on a mixed case DELIVERY Free locally or for 3 cases or more, otherwise £9.50 per case. G M T

✪ Star attractions *Burgundy, Rhône, Italy and California are the specialities, and there's a range of grower Champagnes. The company sources its own wines, so it's a list to linger over – and a shop to linger in, especially when they're holding one of their regular tastings.*

Wines of Westhorpe

136a Doncaster Rd, Mexborough, South Yorks S64 0JW (01709) 584863 FAX (01709) 584863 E-MAIL wines@ westhorpe.co.uk WEBSITE www. westhorpe.co.uk HOURS Mon–Thu 9–9, Fri–Sat 9-6 DISCOUNTS Variable on 1 case or more DELIVERY Free UK mainland (except northern Scotland) MINIMUM ORDER 1 mixed case. M

✪ Star attractions *An excellent list for devotees of Eastern European wines – especially Hungarian and Romanian, as well as some Chile,*

Australia and South Africa, all at reasonable prices. From Hungary there's Kékfrankos, Kékoportó and Tokaji, as well as Szekszárdi Cabernet Franc and Budai Sauvignon Blanc, both at £3.99.

Wright Wine Co

The Old Smithy, Raikes Road, Skipton, N. Yorks BD23 1NP (01756) 700886 (01756) 794175 **FAX** (01756) 798580 **E-MAIL** bob@wineand whisky.co.uk **WEBSITE** www.wine andwhisky.co.uk **HOURS** Mon–Fri 9–6; Sat 10–5:30; open Sundays in December 10.30–4 **CARDS** MasterCard, Switch, Visa **DISCOUNTS** Wholesale price unsplit case, 5% mixed case **DELIVERY** Free within 30 miles, elsewhere at cost. **G**
✪ **Star attractions** *South Africa, Australia and Alsace look good, but it's a pretty comprehensive list, so you'll also find short(ish) but well-chosen selections from Burgundy, the Loire, Portugal, Italy, Argentina – and everywhere else.*

Peter Wylie Fine Wines

Plymtree Manor, Plymtree, Cullompton, Devon EX15 2LE (01884) 277555 **FAX** (01884) 277557 **E-MAIL** peter@wylie-fine-wines. demon.co.uk **WEBSITE** www.wylie finewines.co.uk **HOURS** Mon–Fri 9–6 **CARDS** None **DISCOUNTS** Unsplit cases **DELIVERY** 1 case £20; 2 cases £11; 3–4 £6; 5 or more £4.50 **EN PRIMEUR** Bordeaux. **C M**
✪ **Star attractions** *Fascinating list of very old wines. Bordeaux from throughout the 20th century – there are umpteen 1961 clarets and a decent selection of serious wines from every vintage since. Red and white Bordeaux are the top performers on this list, but there are also a few Rhônes and Burgundies, plus ports going back to 1912, Madeiras to 1870.*

Yapp Brothers

The Old Brewery, Mere, Wilts BA12 6DY (01747) 860423 **FAX** (01747) 860929 **E-MAIL** sales@yapp.co.uk **WEBSITE** www.yapp.co.uk **HOURS** Mon–Sat 9–6 **CARDS** MasterCard, Switch, Visa **DISCOUNTS** £5 per case on collection **DELIVERY** £5 one case, 2 or more cases free. **C G M T**
✪ **Star attractions** *Rhône and Loire specialists who really know their way around these regions. They also have some of the hard-to-find wines of Provence (Bunan/Ch. de la Rouvière, Richeaume, Trevallon), plus Charles Schléret from Alsace – oh, and two interlopers from Australia (Jasper Hill and Neagles Rock).*

Noel Young Wines

56 High Street, Trumpington, Cambridge CB2 2LS (01223) 844744 **FAX** (01223) 844736 **E-MAIL** admin@nywines.co.uk **WEBSITE** www.nywines.co.uk **HOURS** Mon–Sat 10–8, Sun 12–2 **CARDS** AmEx, MasterCard, Switch, Visa **DISCOUNTS** 5% for orders over £500 **DELIVERY** £7 first case, £4 subsequent cases, larger orders negotiable **EN PRIMEUR** Australia, Burgundy, Italy, Rhône. **G M T**
✪ **Star attractions** *Fantastic wines from just about everywhere. Think of a region and you'll find the best wines on Noel Young's list. Australia is a particular passion. There's a famously good Austrian list, some terrific Germans, plus beautiful Burgundies and Italians.*

Who's where

COUNTRYWIDE
Aldi
Asda
L'Assemblage
Australian Wine Club
Bat & Bottle
ChateauOnline
Co-op
High Breck Vintners
Justerini & Brooks
Laithwaites
Lay & Wheeler
Liberty Wines
Majestic
Marks & Spencer
Morrisons
New Zealand Wines
  Direct
Oddbins
OZ Wines
Sainsbury's
Somerfield
Sunday Times Wine
  Club
Tesco
Thresher
Vin du Van
Virgin Wines
Waitrose
wine-pages-shop.com
Wine Rack
The Wine Society
Wine Treasury

LONDON
John Armit Wines
Balls Brothers
H & H Bancroft Wines
Berkmann Wine
  Cellars
Berry Bros. & Rudd
Bibendum Wine
Bordeaux Index
Budgens
Cave Cru Classé
Corney & Barrow
Domaine Direct
Farr Vintners
Fortnum & Mason
Friarwood
Goedhuis & Co
Harvey Nichols
Haynes Hanson &
  Clark
Jeroboams
Lea & Sandeman
O W Loeb
Mayfair Cellars
Montrachet
Moreno Wines
Morris & Verdin
Philglas & Swiggot
La Réserve
Howard Ripley
Roberson

RSJ Wine Company
Unwins
Waterloo Wine Co
Wimbledon Wine
  Cellar
The Winery

SOUTH-EAST AND
   HOME COUNTIES
A&B Vintners
Bacchus Wine
Berry Bros. & Rudd
Budgens
Butlers Wine Cellar
Cape Wine and Food
Les Caves de Pyrene
Dodici
Flagship Wines
Le Fleming Wines
Flying Corkscrew
Hedley Wright
Turville Valley Wines
Unwins
Vintage Roots

WEST AND
   SOUTH-WEST
Averys Wine
  Merchants
Bennetts Fine Wines
Great Western Wine
Haynes Hanson &
  Clark
Hicks & Don
Jeroboams
Laymont & Shaw
Mills Whitcombe
The Nobody Inn
Christopher Piper
  Wines
Reid Wines
Savage Selection
Stone, Vine & Sun
Peter Wylie Fine
  Wines
Yapp Brothers

EAST ANGLIA
Adnams
Amey's Wines
Anthony Byrne
Budgens
Corney & Barrow
Roger Harris Wines
Hicks & Don
Seckford Wines
T & W Wines
Unwins
Noel Young Wines

MIDLANDS
Bat & Bottle
Connolly's Wine
  Merchants
Croque-en-Bouche

Gauntleys
SH Jones
Nickolls & Perks
Noble Rot Wine
  Warehouses
Portland Wine Co
Stevens Garnier
Tanners

WALES
Ballantynes of
  Cowbridge
Devigne Wines
Irma Fingal-Rock
Moriarty Vintners
Terry Platt
Tanners

NORTH
Berkmann Wine
  Cellars
Booths
D Byrne
Great Northern Wine
Harvey Nichols
Martinez Wines
Nidderdale Fine Fines
Penistone Court Wine
  Cellars
Playford Ros
Richardson & Sons
Frank Stainton Wines
Vinceremos
Whitesides of
  Clitheroe
Wines of Westhorpe
Wright Wine Co

SCOTLAND
Berkmann Wine
  Cellars
Cockburns of Leith
Corney & Barrow
Friarwood
Peter Green & Co
Harvey Nichols
Raeburn Fine Wines
Valvona & Crolla
Villeneuve Wines

NORTHERN IRELAND
Direct Wine
  Shipments
James Nicholson
Winemark

CHANNEL ISLANDS
Sommelier Wine Co

FRANCE
Millésima
Oddbins
Sainsbury's
Tesco Vin Plus
Wine & Beer World